Jack Micheline

ONE OF A KIND

Ugly Duckling Presse
Brooklyn, NY

FIRST EDITION

LIBRARY OF CONGRESS CATALOGING-IN-PUBLICATION DATA

MICHELINE, JACK, 1929-1998.
ONE OF A KIND / JACK MICHELINE. -- 1ST ED.
    P. CM.
ISBN 978-1-933254-41-8 (PBK. : ALK. PAPER)
I. TITLE.
PS3563.I334O53 2008
811'.54--DC22
                                2008005979

DISTRIBUTED TO THE TRADE BY
SPD/SMALL PRESS DISTRIBUTION
WWW.SPDBOOKS.ORG

FOR INFORMATION ON THIS OR OTHER TITLES, PLEASE CONTACT:
UGLY DUCKLING PRESSE
232 THIRD STREET #E002
BROOKLYN, NY 11215
WWW.UGLYDUCKLINGPRESSE.ORG

NATIONAL
ENDOWMENT
FOR THE ARTS
A great nation
deserves great art.

THIS PUBLICATION WAS
FUNDED IN PART BY A
GRANT FROM THE
NATIONAL ENDOWMENT FOR THE ARTS

Poems & PROSE

Appendix

Introduction to <u>ONE OF A KIND</u>

New York City
February 8, 2008

Dear Jack,

I thought I'd write you a quick note just to let you know that the book you'd been working on for all those years is finally here. In fact, someone is holding the book right now and wondering what I'm going to say about it, about you, about poetry and the world of poetry and where you stand on it. Chances are, this person has heard your name but never read your work, since all of your old books are out of print. All of those love's labor's journals that published your stories and poems in the 1970s are gone, too, and impossible to find no matter where you look. Still, a lot of people have heard of you. When I bring you up, they look off into the distance trying to find your name in lights. Sometimes, I have to admit, they just change the subject. Something you once wrote keeps coming back to me: "I've built this totally false image of myself. It is almost like building something that will grow when I pass on."

You wrote that in a letter to your son, Vince, toward the end of your life. You were talking about how it was getting hard for you to walk into a bar in North Beach, San Francisco, without everyone expecting you to put on a crazy drunken show. You were getting tired of it, yet you kept going to the same bars.

I could be wrong that this is the book you would have wanted, so here's the story. Some time back, Vince contacted me with the idea of doing a book. Actually, he contacted the press that I sometimes work with, Ugly Duckling, through a friend, and I happened to be standing not far down the road. The whole story of the Presse and all the fortuity and heartache it's brought me, I'll tell you another time. What happened next, I called Vince and told him how interested I was; and he invited me to Tucson to visit your archives.

You've got to understand how excited this made me, even when I admit that I don't think I had ever read a poem by you. Talk about crazy! You see, it has everything to do with that thing you said to Vince in the letter. Even if the image I had in my mind was totally false, I already knew all about you. I grew up in Berkeley, California, and read my first poems out loud in San Francisco at the Café Babar, its door within sight of your old hotel. All of the great poets crammed into that smoky dented backroom of Babar were your brothers and sisters. Poets like David Lerner and Vampyre and the Bubble Lady of Telegraph Avenue, Julia Vinograd. Man, they were a tough crowd.

Now, I don't *think* you ever walked in while I was there, but it could have happened—that was twenty years ago, ten years before you died—but I felt you there, anyway. More than any other poet, you presided in spirit over Babar and North Beach. When you call yourself a Prince in that poem to Charles, "Satellite Communication #3," I know you're kidding on one level, but I think that's sort of how people saw you. They saw you as a Prince whom they didn't have to revere, like a Prince Hal with poetry in the teeth. A lot of people still see you that way.

More than three years passed before I made it to Tucson—but it had to be this way: It took me three years to catch up with my initial buzz. All it was at the beginning was a good hunch that I could make a great book out of your work. A desert island book.

Vince told me that the archives were full of scribbled matchbooks and poems on old racing forms and lost works. He told me he had 20 or 30 crates of papers in storage in Tucson. He sent me a few of your manuscripts and that's where I first saw the title "One of a Kind".

I didn't realize then that these "manuscripts" were copies of the books you were self-publishing throughout the 80s and 90s. They were examples of the actual books that you had assembled to sell, plastic-spiral-bound, as you wandered between New York and San Francisco. The only thing is, they were missing the incredible hand-painted covers that you attached to every book that you sold; so I saw them, mistakenly, as different manuscripts—One of a Kind, Poem from Barcelona, Letter to Kerouac in Heaven—with many poems, stories and drawings appearing in all three books. I'm not sure if you know this, but in some cases you included the same poem twice in a single book! You were making the books fast—taking copies of copies of photocopies of old book pages and copying them a dozen times again. You were copying pages out of old magazines and newspapers where your poems had appeared, and cutting them in with new poems printed on dot-matrix printers. Once, you even threw in a poem by your friend Bob Kaufman. In the process, every book you made was different—a ramshackle Selected Writings with an original painting for the cover (you were definitely one great colorist, Jack). Each book was one of a kind.

I didn't understand this till I opened your archives. I saw, then—I think I can say—exactly what you were doing, your process and where it came from...because I've always done the same thing. You were making books to sell, definitely, on the street and at readings. But you were also trying to assemble the ideal book from all of your past and newly breaking work. Every time you sat down to make a book, you set out to make a great book that flowed together as it should—as a horse race or a river of red wine. That big stack of unsold masterpieces in the dark! They were still alive when I got to Tucson and pried open the plastic crate. They were still alive with your restlessness. Real living treasure.

So I'm at the Silvaer home, hanging out with Vince and his wife, Sheri, and your two grandkids, Dustin and Nicole, but not as much as I want to because I've got two nights and a day to catch your lightning in the paper storm and keep from losing it—two nights and a day was all the time I had…and I have about a dozen crates, about half of the total in storage, since Vince was right: I could get lost on your trail for *weeks* instead of days. And it gets to the point where I can't sleep—I'll dig all day till dawn then take piles of your stuff to bed and keep reading. And I can't believe—I start to go crazy with—how good it is. How fucking unbelievably good your stories are, especially. I'm thinking of *Bolo* right now, and how it reminds me of something someone, maybe a critic, once said: That when you read The Jungle by Upton Sinclair, you're reading an excellent book by an American storyteller, but when you read As I Lay Dying by William Faulkner you're reading a story that might have been told by the Storyteller to anyone from any culture at any point in human history.

And I start wondering, kind of raving, "How could they have *missed* this? Why does Literature consider Jack Micheline a joke if It considers him at all? When he puts *everyone in the dark!* except for Kerouac—and who in Literature would take Kerouac seriously if they could ignore him? Or Henry Miller. But Micheline is right up there with Kerouac and Miller for telling it all, and everything he writes he tries to be great and he is completely himself *always*. He never shows off." —And that's true: You never once showed off in your writing— "He *is* his poem. Look at these beautiful, hilarious poems! What do smart kids have that Micheline lacks? Irony. That's the one unforgivable transgression against literary taste: lack of irony. Why? because American Literature is totally bourgeois, and sincerity is pornographic to the bourgeoisie."

But now I'd call it simpler than that. The bourgeoisie is a bugaboo anyway. So is American Literature. And sincerity isn't a commodity. The people who don't like your work don't like it for their own reasons. You came to realize that you didn't need them, but you also fought off a sense of inferiority your whole life for not being one of them—I mean, for being a self-taught artist who knew he was a poet as soon as he heard the word.

You've run into trouble for sticking to it, not that you had a choice. It's not as if you *decided* to not be a fake. But, like many of the poets who were your friends, you didn't fit into any category and were therefore considered unmanageable by publishers and critics. Despite Kerouac's praise for your poems, you weren't a Beat Poet any more than Bob Kaufman was. Your painting style has been called "primitive" but you learned a lot about your line from your friend Franz Kline. You were a colorist with a brush (actually a box of split-open magic markers) in friendly conversation with Kenneth Patchen and Henry Miller and Paul Klee. You were friends with Charles Bukowski for a long time, and received an insulting letter from his publisher to the effect that you were unpublishable by his press because you were too much like Bukowski—simply because the same things turned you on, in poems and in life. Your story *Skinny Dynamite* got your publisher busted for obscenity in 1968—late enough in the game, you would think, to rate a footnote after "Howl" and The Naked Lunch—but that story went out of print, too. (I'm not sure if you ever read the letter that Allen Ginsberg wrote in defense of your story, where he praised your "precise eye and economical phrasings for concrete particular details of persons, looks, scenes, situations and actions.") You've been called Post-Beat, a member of that group of poets (not really a group) who supposedly followed the Beats (another trick category) as Troubadours—away from the academy and onto the street. Some of that last part makes sense, but my point is that none of these categories appear very useful from a *marketing* standpoint or from an academic one, and anyway you didn't fit in. Poets who depend upon highly competitive grants for survival will ignore anyone who's not playing that game. As an object of criticism your work is a dead end. To have a say, you need to know the rules you're breaking—you need to know them in bed. No wonder you got so drunk at the school dance.

I started drawing up this book on that last night in Tucson. My sense of scale may have been way off, since I know that none of your books were ever published in a large edition, but I made a rule for myself: To stay away from North of Manhattan, your most comprehensive selection of poems—to treat that book as if everyone in America had already read it. But since this wasn't true, I broke the rule and included a few poems that did appear in that book...I couldn't keep out "A Look Back At My Youth".

All I want now is to hear you read that poem out loud to me, but since you can't, I'll read it out loud every time I come across it.

But mostly I stuck to that rule and another one: To go for unpublished work—at least work that I *think* was never published. The list of your published work that Vince gave me seemed pretty comprehensive, but some of my hopefully plum finds may have appeared in very small journals. My guess is that half of the work included here was never published anywhere but in your one-of-a-kind handmade books.

And then there was a third rule: To publish nothing that appeared in <u>Sixty-seven Poems for Downtrodden Saints</u>, the book that Matt Gonzalez edited with your assistance right before you died. But I broke this rule, too. The poem/prose piece "Praise Be to the Original Mind Who Breathes Fresh Air" appears in both books in slightly different forms. I chose to publish the rougher cut that I had encountered many times on my journey through the archives, because I think it's better than the edited version. Maybe this was a dubious choice, since I know that you signed off on the edited piece in <u>Sixty-seven Poems</u>, but your original poem, however slightly different, is *saltier*, and too good to leave out.

Then there was the issue of how to handle <u>Notes of the Lost Cities</u>, the huge unpublished collection of short poems mentioned by you in your interview in the Appendix to this book. Only a handful of these poems have appeared anywhere. It's almost as if you were hiding this book from everyone, knowing that one day, at the final second, it would blow the world back together. For a minute, I almost abandoned <u>One of a Kind</u> in favor of <u>Notes</u>. It's an amazing book with a headlong veer through the New York City of your youth, and it's full of desperate signs Elsewhere and raindrops and real cups of coffee and postage stamps. I couldn't put it down, so I selected a few slices in sequence and hung a couple of solitary notes in the flow of this text. I decided to treat these poems as sketches, leaving out the titles and signaling their passage in the Table of Contents.

This brings up some of my other editorial decisions. In Tucson, I resolved to let all of your misspellings and typos stand, because they were often great. Half the time I couldn't decide whether or not they were intentional. Later, I stepped back from this decision and thought I would correct all typos as well as misspelled words that you spelled *correctly* at other points in your papers. But the method of "silent correction" is an all or nothing proposition. All of the things you save for their idiosyncratic flavor seem artificially precious when you return the next day. A simple explanation was that I was afraid of appearing to be a sloppy editor. As I closed in on a finished draft, I looked for guidance in the larger books whose publication you oversaw. As far as I can tell, the spelling in both <u>North of Manhattan</u> and <u>67 Poems</u> is uniformly correct. In this book, I've chosen to correct all obvious typos and preserved strange spelling where it feels intentional.

<u>One of a Kind</u> is essentially a double-nickels-on-the-dime rendition of one of your handmade books. You often started

with poems and ended with prose and drawings. This book is bell-shaped with the prose block curving up and sloping down in the middle. I cut a few short stories in with the poems, as I'd seen you do—started the book with the "Satellites" otherwise unpublished (as far as I know) except at the front of one of your assemblages. The book should flow backward and forward about the same, like a wave coming back on itself. I loaded it with my favorite selection of your line drawings, almost all of which have never been published anywhere. One of the craziest things was uncovering that big cache of hardbound sketchbooks in one of the crates, with all colors of magic marker soaking through the pages in mirror images—hats, flamingoes, migrating portraits. Holding those books, it hurt to not have the money to publish them.

You'll enjoy one irony, though, and that's that the NEA came up with a big chunk of money for this book, though they turned you down way back when. I know you made a lot of enemies over time, too, but I guess that doesn't really matter anymore. All that matters is what's here and what's coming.

One more thing. I found your note at around 5 in the morning while digging through a vast pile of rubble. Two words

YOU COCKSUCKER

scrawled in blue pen on a scrap of paper.
Thanks, Jack. Same to you.

More soon,
Julien Poirier

p.s. In Tucson I met your ex-wife, Pat. She says she has a big stack of all of the raunchy personals that you wrote to women near the end of your life, and letters back from them, too. She wants to publish them as a book, and I agree, it would make a great book...so keep your bananas peeled.

ACKNOWLEDGEMENTS

Thank you, Vince Silvaer, for your dedication to your father's life's work, and for your total trust in me as an editor. Thank you to the whole Silvaer family, to Sheri, Nicole and Dustin, for your hospitality and friendship and stories about Jack.

Pat Cherkin advised me on this book and told me many stories and opened many lines of approach in the process. Thank you, Pat.

I want to thank Matt Gonzalez, who advised me to do a book strictly of unpublished Micheline. His advice was my guiding principle in making a book that I hope will be vital to Jack's longtime readers and startling to his new ones.

Steve Dalachinsky and Yuko Otomo loaned me copies of Jack's books and told me stories about his roaming suitcase archive full of dirty underwear and girlie magazines, including poems. Steve gave me a priceless tape of Jack performing his poems. Thank you, Steve and Yuko.

Thank you, James Hoff, for buying me a copy of Jack's short story collection, Skinny Dynamite, from which the story *The Purple Submarine* had been carefully torn, inspiring me to include it here.

Thanks to Greg Ford for his 9th-inning pinch-hit copy-editing double.

And thank you, Kailey Moran Poirier, for transcribing virtually the entire manuscript of One of a Kind from an unruly, skewed deck.

Ryan Haley of Ugly Duckling Presse did all of the digital layout on this book, with only my inept assistance to hinder him. No Ryan, no book.

One of a kind

N KENMORE

POWER

Alcohol, economy

PASS 105SINS

RAT PACK

NEGROES cleaning

Cook It Slowly Mama I'm Coming Home

cook it well
stir up the pot
been a gypsy
most of my life
Gypsy blood
wild eyes
too many robots
iron machines
on the long highway
across the sky
cook it well
stir up the pot
tired walking
cheap hotels
concrete carpets
all night cafés
too many robots
iron machines
Monterey finished
Bakersfield too
shopping centers
airplane glue
clouds are changing
country too
polar blears
mental zoo
Monterey finished
Bakersfield too
shopping centers
airplane glue
cook it well
stir up the pot
tired walking
I'm coming home

San Francisco
October 23, 1986

Intercommunication Satellite 1   San Francisco
March 21, 1980
570 Filbert St.

Dear Charles,

      I have come to a come to a decision, about
freedom and responsibility, about loneliness and curiosity,
about greed and more greed. About America and its des-
tiny, about dreams and fantasy, about cats and dogs, about
love and hate, about history and demagogues, about mass
murderers and comic relief, about desire and the fulfillment
of a lifetime is predestined before our birth; do not judge, do
not judge, do not judge, do not judge, and let me be, I did not
seek fame, I did not seek money, I only sought to con-quer
the unknown, the vast territories of the unexplored mind.
No one gives a shit for the artist, Power is respected.

                    I deal in color and truth
                    I deal in unknown quantities
                    I deal in the zodiac
                    I deal in preson and prisms
                    I deal in shit kicking
                    I deal in fear
                    Knowing that fear runs the
                    wheel of the world
                    I cannot deal with cunning
                          hustlers
                          con-men
                          and cliques
                    I can only be me
                    I can only be
                    That is all I can do
                    The best I know how
                    That is all I can be
        Be patient
        It is all coming
        in its own time
        The rainbow of colors in the night
        The rainbow of my dreams
        Be patient
        It is coming like the sun
        in a dark cold day

like a hot iron and a forge
Like going Bannana
Each being is a different species
There is no two fish alike
You turn the knob on the clown
Not on me, The fishtank of your childhood
disturbs me throw the fishtank away and dance
in the street, My car is not in your driveway
Love the crazy Jew
Keep the faith
Keep the faith
Relax
Laugh in your belly
Smile brother it is just beginning
Farewell—Jack Micheline

Satellite Communication Number 2

York City Under Siege

Hunchback Slim ran down Canal Street like a wild crazy
man, he was 6'3" and skinny like a stick. Kangaroo had one
eye and the people of the city rarely smiled. Go home and
be safe. Niggers, Greedy Jews, Middle class opportunities,
rents, downpayments, mortgages, Assholes, Art dealers,
shrimps, pipeline hunters, name suckers, name droppers,
Real Estate Men, Dope Dealers.

On the Bottom of the hill
The sun shines bright
On the Bottom it is dark and cold
We are the brothers underground
We are the brothers All
More Wine
More Wine
Give Us more Wine

Nobody beats this town
The dues are too high
Everyone gets taken
At the age of fifty
taken on a city of fear
three locks on every door

Horses
Horses
Up my ass
Numbers
Numbers
Dames
Dames
Baseball
Baseball
Basketball
Basketcases

The end of Greenwich Village
Sailor Joe

Stanley
Big Mike
Anton
Indian Willie
Rienzi
Replaced by Karp, Castelli, Rosenkranz
Art Literary Establishments
Jews who are not Jews
Gentiles who are Jews
And Jews Who are Gentiles

If you got any heart at all
No one human being can live here
Not One
Agony
Torment & Agony
This is the world and a million sewer rats weeping (Lorca)

All Words Without Truth Are Shallow

New York is loaded with Poetry
Every light is a poem
Every muscle a poem
Every blue face in a bar is a poem
Every Crazy Jew is a poem
Malcalm is a Poem
Harold Goldfinger is a Poem
Perry Street is a poem
Norman Mailer not a poem
There is the business of words
And words without truth is shallow
Don't turn out the lights
They will shine again
Be much good stuff walking alone at night, Charlie it's been
hectic,
I'll keep it short
It takes time to adjust to madness
I'm on the front lines everyday
This is a city of inhumanity of frightened scared people
Everybody feels threatened
Bars make money

Stores make money
Restaurants make money
Race tracks make money
Bees make honey
Ken Kesey makes Honey

Ken Kesey

Ken Kesey was born on a dairy farm outside Eugene,
Oregon, Crazy about tape recorders and electric
parapanellies. A healthy Robust individual who went to
church Regularly and was a Boy Scout. An American
Leprechaun. Kesey knew how to dance at Stanford—
Specialized in Electric Shock Treatment And Spiritual-
Communal Realistic Sexual, L.S.D. Therapy. His family
specializes in producing a rare popular Yogurt in Pleasant
Hill, Ore. Kesey a Jack rabbit novelist wrote *Cookoo's Nest*
three times to imprene manuscript. A man tremendously
driven by a personal mission of a social brotherhood and
cooperation between people. *Sometimes a Great Notion*
was entirely written from typed tapes Recorded on
Buses, Trains, Automobiles, farm houses, bars, street
corners, churches and football games. Totally American
in his roots was inspired by Tom Wolfe and Kerouac and
French and Russian novelists including Balzac, Victor
Hugo, Dostievsky. A Grandesque Rebellion in hipster and
jokester. He married a marvelous woman and had five kids.
He moved from Lahonda to S.F. to Sonoma to back home
in Oregon. Hounded by same cop and government and
phoney politicians of San Francisco, kept his morale and kept
writing. Screwed out of his Movie Rights by Kirk Douglas
and Michael. Finally received an Out of Court Settlement.
Produced poetry festivals in Eugene, Oregon, 1976 and 1977.
Awarded many Awards and prizes after success of *Cookoo's
Nest*. Seems to be the same person unaffected by celebrity
bullshit syndrome. Seems to be a five star Person who went
back to his roots and remained human. The Old Bus he
traveled across country still sits on his farm with his dogs,
cats cows wife kids and Bumble Bees.

May 1, 1980

A DUAL PERSONALITY

STANLEY KOWALSKI

JON HASS

GARY REITHMEIR

JOE VASQUEZ

THE RUNNER

MOTHER comploy
Ambition
ANIMAL
AGressive Personality
SPIRITUAL COP-OUT

selfishness
warmth
KINdness
STUD
ROMANCE
LIGHT
Gambling

A RUNNIER

Ive got what it takes he said
Marry me she said
I can't marry you now he said
I love you she said
Your crazy he said
I want a permanent relationship she said

Satellite Communication #3

Dear Charles:
Received yesterday your checks
I do not ask for your judgment of Jews or Low lifes
I'd appreciate it if you kept your strong opinions to yourself
knowing you, it is impossible.
I want you to know I am my own man
no matter what you think
you can try to buy me, but you cannot be me.
We are not as strong and brilliant as you might be
My weaknesses, shame, doubts, inconsistencies are due to
environmental
quick changes, I am a warrior not an ass kisser.
A saint and a Sinner all in one.
These are hard times now
I am not a young man and I cannot live as an exciting life
as I am accustomed,
What I admire in man is his nobility, his pride. I lack basic
intelligence
I am hard headed, cruel only to myself,
So I ask you to be patient,
I have always been torn between love and hate, Joy and sadness.
Life and Death, life is not a game.
With or without you I will survive
I am a human being, a New Jew,
Self liberating, Probing and Growing.
I left the ghetto many years ago,
Your Snide remarks I do not appreciate.
There are all kinds of Jews but very few individuals.
Some day you'll know who I am.
Go raise your arms to the sky and dance.
Go sing a song.
Laugh an hour without stopping.
There are certain things you cannot do,
Nor do you have a desire to do.
I am a Prince.
I am a Prince.
Prince Micheline
and from now on you treat me as One
I am a Prince.

I am a Prince.
I am a Prince.
You are my adviser and Banker.
You are a friend of the Prince.
When the Prince is happy, you are happy.
I am the Happy Prince visiting the New York nut house,
Frontlines
Frontlines
Frontlines
Frontlines
Go play with your cat
Go kiss the cat
Kiss Sally
I am a Prince
Love Jack

RED

Red is the color of Blood
Red is the color of the Robin's wing
Red is the color of clay
The Glow around Charlie Mingus is red
Red is the color of earth and mountains
Red is a hot color
Red is sensual
there are many shades of red
Bill Saroyan, Henry Miller, Bob Dylan, Charlie Mingus wear
        red hats
Red hats are worn by Tibetan monks
Red is the color of the moon
Red is a fire engine
The red light district is red
Red is a traffic light
Stop when you see red
Sexy women wear red
Red is deep
Demons are red
Peppers are red
When I was young I painted my room red
Planes at night blink red
Airports are red
The monkey is red
Some automobiles are painted red
Red Shoes is a name of a movie
Red is the color of wine
River of Red Wine was the name of my first book
Annis Nin, Charles Bukowski, Allen Ginsberg all have red
        faces
Tomatoes, Apples, Cherries and Strawberries are red
Hot lips are red
Chimneys are red
Farm houses are red
The barns are painted red
Some buildings are red

New York and New Mexico are covered with red
The Chinese are red
The rose is red
Red is the color of violence and passion
The sky over Franz Kline was red
The sky over Kerouac and Mingus and Bob Kaufman was red
The sky over Paris is red
The sky over London is red
The sky over Peking is red
The sky over Moscow is red
The Red River is red
Red is the color of my love so fair
The salamander is red
When Charlie gets mad, his face is red
The teacher's hand is always red
The streets of Calcutta are red
The Prisons are red
The Russians are red
Santa Clause wears red
Some Yo-Yoes are red
The Moon over Miami is red
Vampires are red
The rose is red.

May 8, 1980

BLUE

The sky is blue
My nose is blue
Most Jews are blue
Blue Danube waltz
The blue bottle in the window
Blue coats buy industry
Black is blue
Chicago's blue
Belfast is blue
Detroit's blue
Philadelphia's blue
New York is blue
Shanghai is blue
Rotterdam is blue
Sometimes my ass is black and blue
Blue train coming five o'clock
Blue train coming around the clock
Picasso's blue
Paris 1910
The blue café "Le Metre"
There are fifty-five shades of blue
There are blue birds over the shite cliffs of Dover
The blues are originally American negro folk rhythms
Ma Rainy
Billy Holiday
Louis Armstrong
Scott Joplin
Bessie Smith
Blue
Blue is the color of industry
Blue shirts
Blue pants
Blue brassieres
Blue stockings
There is also the blue moon
The Blue Diamond of South Africa

Chinese Communists wear blue hats
Police and firemen wear blue coats
When you lose you feel blue
When you get beat up you feel blue
Most people walk around feeling blue
It is the sadist's favorite color
Bob Kaufman is blue
Bill DeKooning is blue
Henry Miller is blue
Bill Saroyan has a blue face
Bob Dylan has a blue face
Bill Burroughs is blue
Frank Lloyd Wright is blue
Charlie Mingus and Jack Kerouac have blue faces
Norman Mailer was always blue
Bukowski wears a blue hat
Ferlinghetti's ass has always been blue
One must able to laugh and dance with blue
There is a poet in North Beach called Blue
Blue is the color of feeling strong emotions
It is the color of sadness and reality
Blue is real
I walk down the street with blue suede shoes
The moon is blue.

San Francisco
May 30, 1980

PURPLE AND ORANGE

The purple rage
The riders of the purple stage
Napoleon
Mussolini
Homer
The Purple Gang
The purple sun
Orange is the color of the hills
The Jaffa orange
The Valencia orange
Rajneesh followers wear orange
It signifies purity and belief
Orange is the color of the sun
Orange stands alone
Orange does not hide from anybody
Orange is stronger than yellow
Orange and purple make brown
Orange and purple make the color of earth
Orange is at war with purple
After a person becomes black and blue he becomes purple
Purple is a high and holy color
The world would be better with more purple and orange
Orange and Purple are two brothers
The lady I followed up the street wore purple pants
You can see orange two miles away
Long live orange and purple
Charlie is related to William of Orange
I see a sea of orange
on the coasts of the world
Oranges of Florida
Oranges of Spain
Oranges of California
Oranges of Israel
Orange's blood of Morocco
Orange, orange, lets go orange
Go with God

Orange and purple make the earth
Priests dance in the moonlight
Father Murphy loves Mary
His purple robes of the Middle Ages.

San Francisco
May 18, 1985

17

Welcome
to
DAVID'S REST HOME
FOR OLD WHORES

24-Hour Service   No Dues   All Rooms With View

Our Motto:

☞ "Rest for the wicked"

Angelic doppelgangers
also welcome as temporary
or regular guests

Lyres Restrung

PRAISE TO THE ORIGINAL MIND
WHO BREATHES FRESH AIR

It was attributed to Van Gogh that he said before he shot
himself that there was "No Order in Life". His mind burn-
ing colours, deep reds and yellows opening modern art to
the Twentieth century. Damn the critics, the academies of
organized art, or of abortion. They are on earth to ratify the
status quo. Killers of experiment and imagination. Poor suf-
fering unloved man; the Middle has entered this Art Scene
because there is money in it. A taste of Honey Fame.
O'Submarine
Periscope
Hatches open
Torpedoes away
Zonk another hit
A destroyer amid ships
Blown away to the depths of the sea
It is pleasing like a young virgin sweat and honeycombed
desiring, ready for the plunge. The entrance of birdcalls
and stars.
The weak fall by the side and die. A poet of promise
shattered. A Metropolis rises, falls to the decay and rot
of man and time. Rooms, rats roaches, ribald dances,
Alcohol, siringes, needles, pills, perversion, paranoia.
Dark cities on the hill
wheat on the plain
journals of existence
diaries of moments
recorded in an assertion of will
from that will springs all wisdom
knowledge, poetry, revolution, rebirth
in the end accepted institution...
or madhouse, prison jail, of Baudelaire's
cities of Europe.
If it does not sink, the ship comes home.
To port—Hamburg, Lehavre, Marseille,
Stockholm, Brest, Naples, Paris, Constantinople.
I dreamt I saw a hundred Allen Ginsbergs, naked, reading
Howl in a window at Macy's It is a sad affair what Mod-
ern America does to its poets. Or what happens to poets

in twentieth century America. When Man's God is false
he breaks and dies, the followers die but an original mind
survives. Sherwood Anderson, he had a human face; wan-
dered around the night cities of his youth—the vast Ohio and
broadflat Illinois. The machine age had just come and he pre-
dicted the human blockade in Poor White, his fifth novel that
sorts the pieces and glimpses of a wandering youth. And the
Fiery young angry Erskine Caldwell in his epic piece "Sac-
rilege of Allan Kent" published by a small Maine Print Shop
in 1933. Man alienated from society. America got fat and rich
from resources and war. The true element, the communica-
tion from and with man to man became a hardening process.
The stick ball games are gone, the crap games in the school-
yard, the bonfire in the lot. Mickey parties, lost orgies, even
the baseball players lost their fire. O'fat primitive America.
I blow fire up your asshole. Selby's Tra-la-la done shook 'em
up, done blew a wig off a cat in London too. Bukowski in the
dregs of L.A. blowing sounds for all of us. Let his voice be
heard across the sands and deserts of this nation. Too much
commercial bullshit. Too many Ego's deadwoods posing as
artists. Too many face jobs and nose jobs and clowns. A fire-
bug dark German sleeps on a couch in the next room, writes
all over the world turning people on. The doing and the deed
is the revolution. Like the lazy sun breaking though clouds;
Red are the buildings; Black are the walls. But the Fuck-
ing sun lives on, comes after the night and blows our minds,
Yellow! Praise the original mind that breathes Fresh Air.
Piss on Despair, do ya hear. Adios Baudelaire, Firebug of my
mind, Longshots come home after a long ride!

New York City
April, 1968

20

THE BOTTLE OF WATER

It was a sunny Saturday afternoon in the Spring of 1967. I was reading my poem on the corner of West 8th St. and MacDougal in the heart of Greenwich Village. Reading and singing my street ballads, poems and songs. The sky was blue and clear. It was a beautiful day and a large crowd had gathered around me. I finished my last song and moved through the crowd extending my green hat, accepting their coins and bills, and thanking them for their generosity and kindness. A large man with bright eyes and a white beard extended his hand and handed me a slip of paper with his name and address. He said he was an artist who had a studio up the block and he invited me over for a drink. He wanted to extend his friendship and show me his creative endeavors—painting and sculpture.

The Village was full of poets, painters, dancers, singers, writers, musicians, folk singers, mimes, drifters, lost souls, Italians, Blacks, tourists from the Bronx and Brooklyn. A mixture of Bohemians and Beats, Italians, intelligent, professional people, people struggling to find out who they were. People attempting to say something in a mad frantic world. The Village was a haven for freaks and outsiders and a place where one could be left alone practicing their own rare gifts.

A walk up flights of stairs to the third floor of a flat on West 8th Street, the old man opened the door extending his hand. It was a large flat filled with figurative paintings and sculpture. He had been known in the Thirties and had lived in the South of France for many years. He told me he knew all the famous European artists. His wife was a school teacher.

He opened his large refrigerator. There stood a tall bottle of water. The old man claimed the water was from a magic well in Vermont—a well that is over one hundred and fifty feet deep into the ground. "Have a glass," he said smiling. He poured the water from this large crystal bottle into my glass. I drank it slowly and my eyes began to dance as I rose to my feet dancing. "Let's dance," I told the old man; I was a totally exhilarated. "Indeed this is magic water," I said as the old man and I danced for a solid ten minutes. "Bring up some friends and share your experience," he said.

His paintings and sculptures dancing around the room as music played from a radio in the rear of the flat. I had been a known poet on the fringe of society for years when I left the flat going down the stairs to MacDougal Street. The first person I encountered was Charlie Mingus, the bass player. Charlie and I had been friends for years. "Charlie," I said, "I just drank magic water from a magic bottle this old painter I encountered shared with me. Come have a glass. It's the truth, I'm not nuts. See for yourself," I said smiling. We both walked up the three flights and knocked on the old man's door. He answered the door smiling. "This is my friend Charlie. He would like to have a glass of water also." The old man smiled, seated us down and went to the refrigerator and the large crystal bottle containing the magic water from the well in Vermont and poured three glasses of water. One glass for each of us. Within minutes we were dancing together in the middle of his flat. Indeed the water contained a magic formula.

Many years later after I had moved to San Francisco, in the middle of a jazz concert at the Great American Music Hall, Charles Mingus spotted me in the audience. He had not seen me for years, stopped the concert and said to me, "Remember the old man and the bottle of water." He invited me up on stage to read some poems with him, his face was smiling, indeed he had remembered the old man and the magic bottle of water.

Words from a Rummy

And God loved my child rare flower of angels

I walked in the streets of night
so no one could see my face
and heard beautiful sounds

In
the
rain
of
my
cities
I
shall
walk
forever

I shall go to the corners of my city
and look at the bridges
and hear the waves of the river
the spiral bridges
the lights in the night
the faint cries from the houses
then I will go into the city.
at dusk I raise my voice
my eyes to the sea

Chicago June 20, 1960   11am

I sat down
on the curb
on Wabash Avenue
and cried because
I couldn't believe
the world was so cruel

I went to the park
and cried some more
grass in my eyes
birds in the trees
agony, pain, and more agony
and I knew I was not long for this world

ain't no where to go in this town
ain't no where to go in this town

just walking my poor soul
just walking my poor soul

Charlie was up there
five minutes to God

in the gutter near twelfth street
five minutes to God

People passed me by
five minutes to God

no needles for Charlie
4.15 before dawn

the world is a loser
five minutes to God

The dead know nothing
Do not forget this
There is one war
Beyond all other wars
The individual against society
The starving bird against the winter frost
Behold your beauty poet
It is yours to make and remake
Whatever this world is
It is the triumph of the assassin

Fannelli's Bar

①
It was a quiet bar
before the artists came
A couple of espugs
some truck drivers
three factory workers
a small time hood
a horse player

Some one
on a stool
half asleep
waiters
picture on the
wall

The artists came
prices
The people went
The bad checks
the groupies
and the punks
weeping over a
glass of beer

②
Mike sat on the stool
half asleep
smiled kindly
at the waitress
His son Raymond
was a horse
player
Church
and the dollar bill
Mike knew
how to smile
he was kind to him
he could
Mike took care of business

He hired saints as waitresses
counted his money
and took care of business

Jack Micheline 10/15/82

The Face that Beat Time
for Charlie Mingus

It was somewhere in a loft
Red brick
Across the Brooklyn Bridge
Skinny guys coming out with horns
notes filling the air with birds
Rare birds from everywhere flying filling the sky
Zoot, Chinese checkers, dancing trains
The sky
The sky everywhere
up the thighs of dresses
in hot pants
love sounds, panting sounds, desperate sounds
sounds of night and the half moon
sounds of Georgia and Alabama
sounds of the soaring bird
sounds of ancestors
sounds of cowards
sounds clear and unrelenting
sounds fifty years into the century
sounds clear as water
sounds like the murmur of birds and young children
sounds like the unbelievable moon
And all it takes is to be born again
And all it takes to fly is wings
A chicken with wings into the darkness with a dream
into a dream
out of the cold
in the street
in the park by the trees
out of it like Mario Jorrin
A daydream
a stick forever in a dream
His steps Mousourgsky
his steps flying backwards
his steps American
like Lenny Bruce in Lima, Ohio
like Chinese checkers across the sky
like dominoes

It was only yesterday Charlie
The old Man with the water bottle
In the Frigidaire
The Sculptor, the Painter from the South of France
The summertime in the Village reading poems
A water bottle in the Frigidaire
in a roomful of sculptures and paintings
Showing us the dance he had danced
Showing us the notes across the ocean
Across the bridge
Across the continent
Whoever sits in the prison of the soul
Whoever sits where he sat before
Sits nowhere
like dead newspapers
safe like the middle class in the cemeteries
like the horse that never wins
like the wind no one sees
like the bells no one hears
like the chimney pots of Paris rising in the dusk
like the sand and the sky and the empty horizon
like the snow north of Barcelona
like the unbelievable moon
It is now that the blood races
It is now the eye spots the salamander
The chicken howls
The hen crows
The chicken without wings flying home
home the cities of the universe
Le Havre Marseille New York Paris
San Francisco Constantinople Atlanta
The cat's tail beating out a love poem
on an old couch in a bookstore on Market Street
The eye of a filmmaker frustrated with the toil of economics
The mad painter who cannot sing a song
Colors streaming out like a ship on a voyage
A ship in the sky
Across the dark night like a drunken boat
I dreamt I died blowing a Horn
'O Brother
Moving out across pain
Across the tea party of dreams

I remember how ridiculous we are
Old hats in a closet or the back of a car
I remember the loft in Brooklyn
The Jazz sounds filling the air
The Clarinet wailing into the atmosphere
The dancers dancing into the heavens
I remember the faces strung out on cheap wine
I remember the sounds coming out of the air
I remember the face that beat time

August 25, 1977

Poem Written the Morning After Philip Lamantia's Poetry Reading

Have the time an elegance
to aspire studious learning
scholars interpret facts to fit their hat
wanderer sinner rascal such as I
cannot be protected by the wealthy
mind blazing beat of heart shattered by immediacies and
      circumstance
If man be noble he admits his frailties
and does not assume false status
over lowly creatures of this habitation
If it be protocol to bend to Hearst, Hitler, and Stalin
These dirigibles of evil covered by cold Symmetry and
      Symbology
Then the dollar bill replaces the swastika
The hammer and sickle over the slaves camps of Siberia
truths tainted by lies
and half truths pile up copies in death camps
The Jews of Amsterdam led to the railroad cars by Rabbis
Anarchists of Barcelona rising from the ashes
Mars strength is but a shadow warrior once the blade has
    fallen and the wound too deep
Then the songs of the martyr will be sung in the churches
Your adversaries the inventors of hype
with Rasputin eyes and Merlin's hat
They will love you for your weakness
Your eyes already formed by robots
and body scared by
alcohol, roaches, TV screens, race tracks, tenements,
    flophouses, sunrise, sunsets, Friday night speakeasies
The ships of traders laden by treasure
stolen from Incas and Indians by nations of mercenaries
conjured by scholars and priests of manipulation and cunning
Buzzards, Sparrow, Hawk
nightingales, blue birds, Cajuns
By predators who walk the streets rifling trashcans of the
    talented and fallen
and archives stolen and hidden in libraries
If man kills each other

The birds will survive
If the heart of a bird is bigger than man
Then man should salute the bird
one can only love the wild for its magnificence of moments
A heart is a gypsy given freely and
a panther waiting to strike from the mountains
A toke
a bloke of time
my tortured eyes
puppets, marionettes, juxtapositions, telescopes, binoculars,
          constellations, colored glass bright as diamonds
A sliver of tinsel
sparkling in the winds
'O Eye of elegance and brilliance do not forsake me
Here in the concrete of cities
It is eight in the morning and the engines are racing across
          town
And children are going to school
And the Nut is nobody's right and nobody's wrong
And each one has his or her own truth
Here in the stone citadels of my Mongolian America
And the hospitals and prisons and groans
The bird does not compromise with the air
I have walked the streets of my land out of my head
And the cemeteries are full of good people
And it's just the living that's fucked up
And those who have not walked with me will never understand
I see love lights across the universe

                                        San Francisco
                                        October 15, 1977

Each one got a head

Each one got a heart

Each got a eye ~

Each one got a nose ~

Each one got a little toe ~

Young boys are wet

Broken their eyes. LOVE on their tongues

Bellys full of jelly

Young Girls are mice

APPLE SAUCE

PUSSY WILLOWS

The Hidden Eyeball

Genius is my brother
It is an outlaw
It screams in the night
nervous and fidgety
a flashing star
shooting across the sky
A hot walker
a stealer of third and home
A freak of time
Always ahead of its time
Mediocrity is his enemy
It stands alone triumphant
Einstein
Aaron Copland
James Joyce
Vachel Lindsay
Franz Kline
Charlie Mingus
Charlie Parker
Van Morrison
Houdini
It all hangs out
The shirt and trousers of time
Eye blazed saliva on lips
Its steps crooked
on the way to the mountain
to the city of rainbows
Breeder of Freedom
It seeks new friends
If hidden in dark corners
It dies alone unrecognized
A freak of time
An epileptic
A hunchback
Genius is a hurricane
A tornado
An Aurora Borealis
Alone in the wind
a lost child

in the cities of time
on a lost trail
seeking the mountain of crystal
Genius is a rainbow at dawn
A vibration
A bag of magical beans
Dancing across the world
It makes love to the unwanted
The misfit
The outlaw
The dreamer
The inventor of eyeglasses
The geek in the circus of time
It dances forever
up the mountain
From the North Pole
To the Himalayas
Across the China Wall to down under
on New Zealand
Across Africa
To South America
Across Mexico to Alaska
From Iceland to Lapland
Across Denmark and Finland
Across Russia and the Volga River
Through Afghanistan, India
And Central Asia
Genius is a rare bird
A crooked giant
A five colored pansy
Blowing in the wind
A hidden eyeball
Ready to Pop
Popeye himself
A dance on a crooked leg
A Dervish with five tongues
A piano moving out across the sky
A symphony of dreams
A child's forever
A parade of ragamuffins
The carnival of dreams
The hidden eyeball itself

A horse never caught
The Giver of light and more light
A bird soaring across the sky
A dirge rising above the mountain
Nolde
Van Gogh
Gauguin
Goya
Picasso
Rimsky-Korsakov
Paul Klee
Miro
Modigliani in the Seine
Bob Kaufman bringing rainbows
Sibelius
Corelli
Haydn
Handel
Hieronymus Bosch
Jack Kerouac
Kandinsky
Rimbaud
Baudelaire
The Mojave Desert
A poet in New York
The dusk of cities
The sky over Turkey
A dream in Arabia
A Spirit indefatigable, unconquered
Dancing from graveyards
The Jig of time

Bishop, California
May 11, 1987

Nine hundred birds
flying in the trees
Nine hundred flowers
blooming in the sun
Nine hundred
Nine thousand
Nine hundred million
Birds flying in the sky
forever
Love up kill me JH

White Owl

Demi-Tip

5 CIGARS BLENDED
WITH IMPORTED TOBACCOS

White Owl
Demi-Tip

White *Owl*

White Owl
Owl

White Owl **Demi-Tip**

THESE CIGARS ARE PREDOMINANTLY NATURAL TOBACCO
WITH NON-TOBACCO INGREDIENTS ADDED

U. S. PAT. NOS. 2592553, 2592554, 3076729 AND
OTHER U. S. AND FOREIGN PATENTS APPLIED FOR

White Owl

Demi-Tip

5 CIGARS BLENDED
WITH IMPORTED TOBACCOS

White Owl®

GUS THE BLINDMAN

Gus always wore a green hat as he hobbled in Tina's
Restaurant with his blind-man's cane. Gus was not born blind.
As a child, Gus loved wildflowers, tulips, roses, sunflowers,
and he loved to look at the stars and listen to the birds. He
became blind in an automobile accident two years earlier.
Gus would tell me of his experiences since he became blind.
Punks, gangs, hustlers, predators of society would harass
him. When Gus was young he was a happy go lucky guy. Now
since he had become blind he had become a cynic, a man who
has lost his sense of wonder and sense of romance in life and
in the goodness of living. Life was good when one had money
and one succeeded in becoming a success. Gus still was able to
smile and laugh even with the handicap of being blind.

At breakfast in Tina's we would sit and talk about old
prize fighters we had seen or heard about: Max Bear, Buddy
Bear, Fritzie Zivic, Barney Ross, Benny Leonard, Gus Lesn-
evich, Joe Louis "The Brown Bomber," Wild man Firpo The
Bull of the Campos from Argentina, Two Ton Tony Galento
from Newark, New Jersey Henry Cream, Jersey Joe Wal-
cott, Sugar Ray Robinson, Tony Zale, Rocky Marciano, Joe
Cocker, Sandy Sadler

     Jack Johnson
     Willie Ketchell
     Rocky Graziano
     Benny Leonard
     Gene Tunney
     Jack Dempsey The Manasa Mauler
     Max Schnelling
     Kid Gavilan Cuban Bolo

Beau Jack, Abe Attell, Animal London, Strangler Lewis,
Wild Dog Rembrandt, and the greatest featherweight of all
pound for pound Willy Pep, the winner of 57 straight fights.

     Marcel Cedan
     died in an airplane crash
     Archie Moore
     Joe Villamain
     Muhammed Ali

Mike Tyson
Archie Moore
Jake Lamotta The Raging Bull
The roar of the crowd
the smell of blood, sweat,
piss, and agony of triumph
and the gloom of defeat.

The hours of training and road work.
Stepping into The Ring for the first time.
Knock your opponent down.
Break his ass, hit at the break,
use your knee, your teeth.
Hit in the clinch, spit in his face,
crawl like a dog.
Curse the Referee,
The Priest

Your mother lied
Your father lied
The preacher lied
The teacher lied
The rabbi lied
Kiss the ass of the rich
Suck a watermelon

Lead with the right
Swing the bolo
         a roundhouse right
Winning is the name of the game.
Sweep the bar of all the money.
Blondes in the first row.
Streetcalls from Bronx rooftops
Brooklyn crybabies
The drums of Harlem
Lovers in Bronx Park
Take Phelan Bay Line
The Dyre Ave. Shuttle
Joe Ryan on second base
Lefty Gomez pitching a two-hitter
Left jab to the nose
Snot from your nose and brain

Iron Man Mike
Bobby Miller laughing
New Orleans is going crazy
Circle your opponent
Swing from the bleachers
A roundhouse right to the head
Stay angry.
This world's a put up job
Most people suck
Slave to the boss
No mind of their own
Most people lost souls of the universe
Worry what their neighbor says

Believe in the newspapers
Watch T.V.
Cry in barrooms
Never get enough
Most are scared to death to move their left toe
Most people in this world play the game
Lead with the right
Kiss the fat girl on the bus.
Most people never found out who they were,
Never even had a chance to find out

The wheel in the sky
The man with the hat
turning the wheel.

Gus would laugh at my attempt to tell jokes. One day he
never showed up for breakfast. Milly the Russian waitress
said he had passed away in his sleep on Sunday. I hoped he
died quickly and had a beautiful dream and there was little
pain. It was all over for Gus the Blindman.

Willy Pep
Artie Klang
Billy Beltram
Jake Lamotta
Benny Leonard
Willy Ketchell
Rocky Graziano

Jack Johnson
Gus came in swinging
A left to the head
A shot to the nose
A right to the jaw
A flick to the lip
Another left to the head
A roundhouse right to the mouth
A wild left to the face
Another to the ear
A right to the head
A left cross to the jaw
A stinging right to the left of the face
A bolo to the jaw
Knockout
The roar of the crowd no more.

June 19, 1992

Those on the road
Those with dream
Those who will never
            give up
Those who are ~~leaving~~
            leaving to one
Those perplexd
        Agonized
        wacked out ~~the~~ the
we are   sun   To Have
all the sun   ~~confused~~
~~took it~~   we all are one
this   Your   are   Surone
world   me
is   This world is ~~one~~ one
one   Those with ~~rainbow~~
Those   Your are the sun
with   we ~~is one~~ Stale the
wonder   sun   sun and the moon,   sun
you are   are brothers
        ~~are one~~   !!!
The   We are ~~one~~ other
    sun the moon are brother

TIGERS IN THE SKY

The night before there was a high moon, the day the rattlers cried and the buses went on strike and the touts hustled for coffee and fare go to the track, I was in my gambler's mood in a gambler's earth and was living in the middle of concrete of cities, while the steamshovels dug up the earth on Market Street and greed and fear hung inside the people on the buses. In cities where poets have an urge to die hearing the death rattle of cobras over the Santa Cruz mountains. In cities where the weepers weep and cryers cry and dreamers die. The eye to behold the sway of buttocks of young girls walking through the streets. A bright orange sweater covering a pair of big breasts. When sensuality screamed through the streets. A young lady with a wild hat pulls up her skirt showing the pink of her thighs. A city full of sensuality and dreams while the sway and the movement of young girls and color slit the air and sky. Crazed with drink the night before, racing through the North Beach streets of lost bohemians and forgotten beats and Jazz musicians. The dreams of money and power and piles of green dollars floating in the sky. The mountains rising from the earth. To hold in one hand the whole world of cold steel and giants. The dreams of Queens and horses racing through the stretch. The sky red and golden after a rain. To beat the machine. To beat the power that builds the prisons and bridges and madhouses. To wage war with hope and luck against the cold steel of man and cities and the machine itself. The possibility of what could be and never is. The dream of kings in the eyes of charwomen that each one is a prince instead of a pauper.

The day had come and I was ready, blue skies overhead and the sun breaking through the fresh cool morning air. The day of the $50,000 Added Vallejo Stakes. I had been going to the track for two days in a row and I was down to my last hundred. The desire for action. To move with the horses and the crowd. I had come to play one horse and one jockey in the featured race, Fresno Star with Gonzales up. Saturday is a madhouse at the track, like Times Square

on a Saturday Night. Blacks and kids and long lines wait-
ing for beer and coffee and cigarettes, the workers in from
the factories and plants and mines. The families looking
for kicks, the lost and the dreamers, the alcoholics and the
runners and the true believers, the racing form players, the
Number players. The weegee board freaks and psychics
and touts and the rich and the well bred just killing time in
the clubhouse. The show players and the professional gam-
blers and the crazies and the crippled and the freaks and
the ones who live and die on luck. The blind and the deaf
and the dumb and it was Saturday and I was going out of
my mind. I played the double and lost. And in the third race
I spotted orange Moon, a drop down in class who lost his
last race at one mile by twenty five lengths going into a six
furlong race going off at 22-1 and I put ten on his nose to
win and he won flying through the stretch paying $44 for 2
dollar bet and I was ahead two-twenty and I was flying and
feeling loose and easy and I dropped it all back and more
on the next four races and I was down to my last fifty and
the horses were parading in the paddock area. And I took
a slug of rock and Rye. I had come to play Fresno Star with
Gonzales up. Whisky bottles and losing tickets on the floor
whirling in a slight breeze and the horses in order of their
post position were as follows:

NUMBER

one	BRAVE WARRIOR	2-1
two	ACKNOWLEDGE ME	11-1
three	GOTTA GO	15-1
four	BLUE SIERRA	17-1
five	DOMINO DUNGEON	35-1
six	YELLOW SEA	60-1
seven	FRESNO STAR	9-1
eight	BEN MOSES	5-2
nine	TOP DOG	4-1
ten	FLAMING RED	3-1
eleven	FATHER GROTTO	99-1

A mile and a sixteenth. The $50,000 Added Vallejo Stakes.
I go to the window and bet $50 to win on number five,
Fresno Star, and the bell rings and they're off.

Around the first turn into the back stretch Fresno
Star out of the pack like greased lightning goes to the
front followed by Yellow Sea, Gotta Go, Brave Warrior,
Acknowledge Me, Ben Moses, Top Dog, Flaming Red and
Father Grotto trails the field. At the half-mile pole Flam-
ing Red comes up to challenge Fresno Star still leading the
pack. Past the three-quarter pole Top Dog and Ben Moses
begin to move from the outside, Acknowledge Me com-
ing on. Around the last turn one-sixteenth of a mile to go.
It's six horses nose to nose across the track. Fresno Star,
Gotta Go, Acknowledge Me, Yellow Sea, Flaming Red and
Top Dog and coming from the outside is Father Grotto, the
horses noses apart, neck and neck through the stretch. A
cloud of dust rising from their hoofs across the finish line. A
photo finish. The crowd is going crazy. A mad roar of fifty
thousand fans jumping up and down like pygmies and mani-
acs screaming at the top of their lungs. The numbers light
up on the board: it's Fresno Star, Flaming Red and Top
Dog, Father Grotto coming from nowhere to take fourth.
Fifty to win on Fresno Star. I go to the cashier's window
waiting to be paid off. I give my ticket to the cashier: num-
ber five, Fresno Star. I scream I bet Fresno Star. Fresno
Star is number seven. Number five is Domino Dungeon.
Sorry, wrong number, he says. Wrong Number. I bet the
right horse but the wrong number. Shit Man. You must be
nuts. I bet Fresno Star. I told the guy to give me Fresno
Star number five, wrong number wrong horse, wrong day
blue sky overhead. I get out of line and leave the madhouse
called the track and get on the bus going anywhere away
from the track. It is getting dark. Dusk is coming over
Berkeley. I get off the bus, walking on and on into the haze.
Past the trees and houses, the sounds of hoof beats and
words springing from my head
Topracaloo
Brenda Sue
Orange Moon
Buggy Ride, Loaded Freight, Sweet Mary, Hopacaloo,

Sweet Sue, Chicken Red, Water Bug Driving Rain Castle
Dawn, I'm so blue Fresno Star, gone to heaven, Larry too,
Larry too Larry too
on into the night
it begins to rain
the sounds of hoof beats in my brain
out over the cities and into the plain
Larry Too
Larry Too
Larry Too
Larry Too
Larry Too

San Francisco
July, 1974

BLUE NOSE WAS 50-1

Blue Nose was 50-1 ready for the glue factory. I had been
playing heavy and into the loan sharks for over two grand.
I had already hocked everything of value I could get my
hands on and I had lost that also, and had borrowed from
all available means possible at my disposal. I had lost by all
conceivable means photos, disqualifications, stupidity and
greed, and playing a lost trade on hope and luck and num-
bers and dreams. I had given it all I had for the last push
and plunge. I was getting seedier every day, uncombed hair,
holes in my shoes and socks, tired from pink eye and no sleep,
walking the streets writing down license plate numbers, and
counting the stars. To find the right number, the combination.
The winning horse at the right odds, just to get even and not
to put my life in jeopardy to the loan sharks who had already
given me a deadline for repayment of funds due them, accord-
ing to a mutual agreement which was due on Saturday, April
19, at midnight. The tidy sum of $2,200 dollars, to be paid in
cash, or suffer the consequences and embarrassment of my
demise. In other words, in more realistic dialogue, I would
be done in by an unscrupulous bunch of cutthroats called the
boys or mob, who were efficient at the work of their profes-
sion. The pound of flesh and bone they needed for the moneys
due them, they would do me in without the slightest hesita-
tion and take my life like a flicker of an eyelash. To say the
least, I was in a frantic state of annoyance, fear, and the very
terror of my possible non-existence. I could not run or disap-
pear from these unscrupulous buggers.

It was already too late, I was already too deep in the soup
and the action of gambling had already possessed my very
being, the agony of defeat and total wretchedness of my
condition dragging my body and soul down the drain of
agony way, I was a jumping bean and a yo-yo. A hot spotlight
beaming across the ages. A hot animal totally desperate as
a tyrant breathing his last minute. To say the least of my
predicament, I was in desperate straits. A wild animal on
the rocks breathing heavy as the hand of the clock ticked the
seconds, minutes, hours of my very existence on this planet
Earth. I had begged fifty dollars from a crippled girl, actu-

ally going down on my knees, begging for the last chance to try to even the score. So down on my luck, I looked pathetic. I could have moved the Pope to charity at the wail of my depravity. I even saw a picture of my mother and son in my dreams, knowing I would never get to heaven playing the horses and receive the bags of gold as a winner. I needed the action, the pain, the suffering and excitement like a wino needed wine, and a poet needed images. To tear from myself the remaining links to the earthly plane. To escape boredom and restraint. To remove my link from reality to an unreal plane. To be at the Top and Bottom at the same time. To be nuts like a wild wind. To fish blind in the dark night looking for gold covered by bandages in the rain. To find the last gold fish in the pond. This need of action my gambler's life. To be a whistle in the wind, lost and groping on a windy night. A speck of dust in the wind of time. A drunk sailor in the cities of night, groping for any touch gentle as a leaf in a leafless plain and all I had left was a stab in the dark.

It was Saturday, and I took the bus to the track. The track was soft after a hard rain. The blacks weaved in and out of the lines. Small children climbed the fence to look at the horses, I pulled my handkerchief and sneezed walking up and down like a maniac. I had lost ten on the Double and was down to my last forty. The sun finally came out.

Blue Nose was 50-1 and out of a glue factory.
Night Flight had an apprentice jockey
Artful Dodger was three times second
George Lemon was coming up in class after winning
Loose Larry once lost a shoe
Brown Bronco was going down in class
High Stocking was a good looking horse
Noble Roman was overdue
Seven Beauties came close a week before
Mt. Logan was a shiny dark horse
Sister Sierra showed some class the year before
Moon Glow hadn't won in four years

It was a $5,000 dollar claiming race for fillies and mares, purse $3,5000, distance six furlongs. The Tote Board read as follows:

No. 1 – Blue Nose   50-1
2 – Night Flight   19-1
3 – Artful Dodger   3-1
4 – George Lemon   2-1
5 – Loose Larry   7-1
6 – Brown Bronco   5-2
7 – High Stocking   11-1
8 – Noble Roman   4-1
9 – Seven Beauties   9-1
10 – Mt. Logan   60-1
11 – Sister Sierra   15-1
12 – Moon Glow   99-1

I watched the horses as they paraded around the paddock. I gave each one a good look as they walked around the ring. I was so tired they all looked the same to me. I began taking to myself. "Lord, give me a sign, Lord." A hunch, a dream. The sun was out. The horse players weaved in and out. Losing tickets blowing in the wind. Dope sheets, dreamers, antibodies. Dreamers, Hustlers, Touts, Sharpies, Greed, and the Big Kill. The horses were on the track. Horse Number 10, Mt. Logan, shook his head at me and looked me straight in the eye. Mt. Logan from Rialto, an out of town track, Blue Nose was 50-1. Moon Glow 99-1, Mt. Logan 60-1. I needed a long shot, but which one was it? I could not hesitate any longer, I could see the goons working me over. My son and mother in my dreams. It was one minute to post time. I started to shake and sweat. The horse that gave me the sign, Mt. Logan at 60-1, that was the one. I ran to the window. Forty Dollars to win on Number 10, Mt. Logan. I pulled my last forty dollars out of my pocket and paid the teller, receiving my ticket. Forty dollars to win on Mt. Logan. With the sound of the bell, the flag was down, and they're off! Noble Roman shot out of the gate like a gun taking the lead. Night Flight followed a half a length away, Sister Sierra a close-up third, followed by High Stocking, George Lemon, Loose Larry, Artful Dodger, Seven Beauties, Brown Bronco, Mt. Logan, Blue Nose and Moon Glow trailed the field. Noble Roman keeps the lead approaching the far turn, George Lemon moving up with Brown Bronco. Night Flight is losing ground with Sister Sierra, Mt. Logan goes to the outside Sixth, followed by Loose Larry, Blue Nose and Moon Glow,

around the turn and into the stretch, a sixteenth of a mile
to go. George Lemon takes the lead, Brown Bronco coming
on, Sister Sierra sneaking in on the inside, Mt. Logan un-
der a head of steam moving to the outside, with Blue Nose
and Moon Glow making their move into the stretch. It's six
horses, noses and heads apart, across the track. The crowd
is going crazy. "Come on, Mt. Logan! You skinny bastard,
come on. Move that horse Benny Carlos, move it!" They ap-
proach the finish line, six horses across the track. A Blanket
Finish. George Lemon, Brown Bronco, Sister Sierra, Mt.
Logan, Blue Nose and Moon Glow. Six horses across the
track, crossing the finish line, heads and noses apart. A
photo finish! An Inquiry Sign goes up on the board, blinking
like a spotlight on a dark night. The jockey, Benny Carlos,
falls off the horse, his body lying on the ground. Shit, Man,
what happened? Mt. Logan is still running, the Inquiry Sign
still blinking. The numbers light up on the board. It's No.
4, No. 10, and No. 1. George Lemon, Mt. Logan, Blue Nose.
Number 4, George Lemon, is blinking. Shit, I got a chance.
Please, God. Please, God in Heaven, pull it down, move it,
Lord. They remove No. 4 off the board, for drifting up in
the stretch. No. 10 goes up. Moon Glow gets second, Brown
Bronco third. I got a winner! Shit, I won $128.80 for a $2
bet, Benny Carlos gets back on the horse, smiling. He's all
right. Mt. Logan won. Whatta' ride, man, whatta' race! I
won. I won. My mother's face, my kid. I kiss the stars. I'm
even. I won. I won. I won! Viva Liberty, Viva Benny Carlos,
Viva me. Viva Mt. Logan, Blue Nose was 50-1.

San Francisco
April, 1977-1981

THE
MAGICIAN

THE PRINCE

It was one of those parties in the Monkey Block, on a rainy Sunday night.

The poets were strung out on pot and wine and speed, and did not complain of a chaotic life. It was in the late fifties, and Grant Avenue was a Mecca of lost Bohemians, artists, poets, and jazz musicians, wanderers, freaks and lost souls who had arrived from across the country to get it on. Lenny Bruce was appearing on Broadway, and Howl had already been written, and poets sat above the Bagel Shop underneath the Zen Tree. John Richardson the red-headed albino spade poet had already finished his pint of wine. Bernie was walking up and down like a maniac. Sally took off her blouse and started dancing to the sounds of the skinny clarinet player Bill Bosio. He was so frail and skinny it looked like he had not eaten in three weeks, and there he was blowing his ass off in the wind and stars. The sound of a crooked horn disappearing into the night sky. Word had gotten out and people were appearing from the cheap hotels and alleys and cold water flats and rooming houses of North Beach. Some of the ladies had ran away from home carrying On the Road under their belts. There was always plenty of wine and bread and cheese, and bodies started dancing, shifting their legs and arms moving to the beat of the jazz and drummers.

And when Bobby came in, the place lit up with a magnetic energy. He had spent too much hard time in the Apple. Bobby ran to the center of the loft, moving his feet with his deep sensitive Creole eyes and his fingers arcing into the night sky. He began a poetic riff with the tenor man in a spontaneous exhilaration, of bop energy of the street he had liberated into a carnival of dreams.

Mona with long dark hair started taking off her over-abundant clothes. The Poet started his spontaneous rhapsody in blues and bop.

Shoo Be Doo
Wacky Waw
Doo me Maw
Americka Wa
     Slinky koo

Lama Dama Shoo
Lakky Lakky Loo

Skoome Buckeroo
Imme Jimmy

Skinny Koo
Lappito Loo,
Lappidy Boo
Linky Loo
Dinky Loo
Slinky Larry Loo
Hoppidy Linky Dinky
Minsky Da Doo
Wacky Jew
Wacky Jew
Ebony Sue
Quacky jack
Ebony Sue
Koo La La La Loo
Koo La La La Loo
Doomy Koo
Doomy Koo
Doomy Koo
Subway rides railroad trains
Americka Dollar Boo
Slimy Goo
No more pain
No more rain

Gentle rain
A hundred flicks
A thousand clowns
Hustling night
Gentle rain
No more pain

Into the sky
Seventeen moons
Skoo Be Doo
Doo Ma Lal
Doo Ma Lal

No more pants
Lost my keys
Orleans Rag
No more shorts

BOLO

Bolo was born blind and deaf but not dumb. He was born
of poor parents in a shacktown on the outskirts of Mexico
City. At night the wild sounds of the champas sprang out
into the sky. He had learned to walk only with the most diffi-
culty only with his yellow and black cane. The other children
laughed at him and played jokes on him. In the shacktown
everyone hustled. The old man Dari was Bolo's friend. He
had given Bolo an accordion as a present on his tenth birth-
day. Bolo struggled hard and in a year learned to play the ac-
cordion well. Bolo had never saw birds and old man Dari told
him about birds. Bolo began to whistle bird calls from his
imagination. Bolo had an ear for music and learned to play
the accordion well. The accordion had become a good friend
of his. Bolo would stand on the corner near the champas and
play the accordion and whistle bird calls. Children followed
him in the streets and people would put money in his tin cup.
Bolo lived alone for his father and mother had deserted him
when he was nine. Dari and the blind girl and the children
that followed him was his only friends. Yolanda was a short
indian girl and she was born blind. When old man Dari died
Bolo cried all night long for he was Bolo's best friend. Bolo
and Yolanda gave the last of their savings to give Dari a
decent burial. Yolanda loved Bolo and Bolo loved Yolanda
and so they lived together. Yolanda helped Bolo dress in the
morning. Bolo and Yolanda slept together and made love. In
the shacktown everyone was poor and everyone hustled. Ev-
eryone hustled to survive and life was a continuous struggle.
Bolo played the accordion and whistled bird calls. The chil-
dren of the champas followed him in the streets. The accor-
dion danced and the sun shone in the sky. It was summer and
the earth was warm and the trees were green and growing.
Bolo stood on the corner near the champas and whistled bird
calls. It was a good day for Bolo, many coins were dropped
into Bolo's tin cup. A gang of tough boys followed Bolo. The
sun no longer shone in the sky. Darkness had come quickly
over the champas. Bolo's tin cup was full with coins. Bolo
leaned on his cane and walked through the field of flowers on
his way home to the shack. The gang of tough boys sprang
out of the darkness. They pounced on Bolo knocking him to

the ground. They laughed as they punched and kicked Bolo on the ground. Bolo swung his cane blindly at the boys. With all his strength he swung and cursed hitting the leader of the gang with his cane. The leader grabbed a loose rock and crashed it down against Bolo's skull. Bolo's blood streamed from his wound into the dry earth. Bolo's body lay limp on the ground. The gang disappeared into the night. Bolo's accordian torn to shreds laying on the ground next to him. The tin cup lay empty. The wind blew against the field of flowers. It began to rain. The music came from out of the darkness from a nearby carousel. The wild horns from the champas sang into the night. The sounds of rain hit against the dry earth. The field of flowers blew wildly in the wind. Yolanda waited for Bolo to come home. The children dreamt of Bolo and the sounds of birds. The white flowers waved in the darkness that was night. The rain poured down and the wind rose out of the field. And the carousal kept turning and Bolo was dead, deader than a dead dog.

THE PURPLE SUBMARINE

Scarlet was tall and skinny and looked like an elf. Her tight skirt and the movement of her buttocks as she slowly swished down the street. Her silk undergarments trimmed in white satin. Ruby lipstick on her profound succulent lips. She had lived seventeen years and two months on this habitation called the planet earth. She was born of male gender with the characteristics of a female, in a poor white honky slum. She was attracted to female clothes and the male cock. By accident and curiousness of youth, she began sucking at eleven. It was fun and exciting especially when wet Freddy popped and came; amid the bright stars and lights of the city and hearing the voices of the angels on the radio. It was not easy to learn and to do it well was hard work, and it was also known in the vernacular of the working class as blow jobs and there were many men who desired to be blowed and were willing to pay for it. Scarlet learned to tongue it slowly and gently but forcefully. Go up and down on it, to yo-yo it. To be known as a queer or a freak was not an easy way to live.

To be born a queer in a macho world and a macho earth. To be made fun of and the butt of ridicule. To hide in restrooms and Johns and closets; putting on clothes stolen in shops and bought in second hand stores. And Scarlet's own father Pinky, brung up on beer and baseball and football and working for a small salary and cursing and hating life because they were poor. Scarlet knew in her heart she was a lady. She practiced simple delicate gestures with her hands and eyes. Scarlet disciplined herself like a lady at finishing school. Scarlet's father Pinky loaded trucks at the Teamsters warehouse and liked hillbilly music and drank beer and was a loud mouth drunk. Scarlet's mother Lulu was a cripple who went to church and had a compassionate heart; she lived in the world of dreams and the Zodiac and was considered slightly mentally retarded. Scarlet felt out of place at school, she would look out of the windows and dream of balls and cock, and streams and mountains and buttercups. Like every true lady's dreams: Scarlet fell in love with Skinny Lenny. Lenny who was also a queen. Skinny had a furnished room near Polk Street. They dressed in each others clothes and sucked each other off. Each taking turns, learning the delicate art of blowing. At fifteen Scarlet became an embarrassment to her parents. She was caught blowing a friend in the men's room by the old geezer the Biology teacher, Hans Pacard, who forcefully pushed Scarlet's face into a toilet. Mr. Pacard brought Scarlet to the Principal and her parents were summoned to school. Their son Scarlet stood in stoned silence amid the screaming and accusations. His parents would not believe their son was a fag, a freak, a cock-sucker, a piccadilly, a queen, a god forsaken homo. His parents acted as if the world had come down on their heads. How the fuck could they have produced a fruit? Amid the earthiness and brutality of their American hillbilly lifes! Scarlet, a flower amid the drug heaps of an Oakland slum. At the age of fifteen Scarlet had a body of an angel, her long red hair and freckled face. She looked so much like a woman it was a crime. She had cock and balls. Scarlet ran away from home.

Scarlet moved in with her old friend Lenny. Lenny had a fantastic wardrobe, closets full of dreams, scarves, blue and green and fuscia slips, white, black and tan garter belts. All kinds of hot colored panties, slim styled dresses. New pumps and uplifts from Frederick's and an assortment of wild hats, perfumes and necklaces, false eyelashes, rouge, powder, and assorted lipsticks and nail polish, thin alligator belts and flesh-tone sheer stockings from the Orient, and an assortment of wigs that would blow out the moon.

Scarlet had the face of an angel. She was so beautiful. Scarlet needed money. Scarlet knew a lot of truck drivers were fags and they liked to be blown.

It was a truck stop in the California desert. The truck drivers waited for Scarlet. Scarlet wore lavender panties. They waited for her tongue on their working man's cock. The men who drove the big ass trucks, fifty trucks lined up in a row. Scarlet went down on them all, and sucked them off with her young lips. They came in her mouth and she received money for her acts of kindness. Nine hundred bucks in one night. Scarlet's lips swollen purple, and her knees black and blue. One son of a bitch was epileptic. And Scarlet's mother reminding her to beware of the men in the black robes.

Scarlet remembered the faces of the cops and bulls at the central station laughing at her clothes and female characteristics. Betty Boop would have been proud. They threw

Scarlet in with the women and out across the desert the truck drivers talked of Scarlet's lips. And they kept talking as the shooting stars crossed the Zodiac.

Nine hundred bucks in one night. She took the money, sharing and giving it to her friends and buying more wild clothes. The best seats at the Winterland and Fillmore to hear Janis and Jimi. She would dance all night.

She was thrown in with a bunch of common prostitutes and the bulls laughed at the hustlers and queers. Scarlet sucked and licked Harold's balls. The big bruiser moaned and groaned. Harold, the Teamster delegate with big nose and twisted eyes, the go-gettem' kid himself, Harold the Horse, leader of the rah-rah and bully boys, these men who led the cheering sections at the Oakland Stadium, the men who believed what they read in the sport pages and headlines of newspapers.

Each one who thought he was better than any other. This was the beginning of greed and the animals never understood. And the faces of the cops at the central station laughing at the queens at the line-up put Scarlet in with the women.

And the other drivers kidded Harold, he was sucked by a fruit. The big macho was sucked by a fruit. It burnt Harold up, this big American man was sucked by a queer. And the next time Scarlet showed up he would get even. The torment and rage in him, football games and union meetings and getting the other drivers into line. All week long Harold kept the rage inside of him waiting for the moment to strike back. It was long after midnight when Scarlet showed up at the truck stop. Scarlet wore lavender panties. Fifty trucks lined up in a row. Harold sitting smoking a cigar on the first truck. Scarlet gave Harold a long sweet kiss touching his cock with her gentle hand. Her long red hair and flashing eyes. Her lips going down on fat Harold, sucking till he came. And then Harold screaming and ripping off Scarlet's clothes calling her a fruit and a cock-sucker. Harold threw Scarlet in back of his cab and grabbed the tire iron screaming she was a fag, he was sucked by a fruit, hitting away at Scarlet's head until she lay dying and already dead. Harold still screaming that he was a man and carrying her body out to the desert with a shovel to throw the remains into the earth and sand. The stars danced across the Zodiac. The other drivers still laughing waiting to be sucked and blowed. Scarlet was better than the mayor's wife and the magistrate's wife and the Alderman's wife, and the police chief's wife couldn't even suck a lollipop. I remember Scarlet spinning out in the night, walking down Folsom Street her face and eyes disappearing into the darkness.

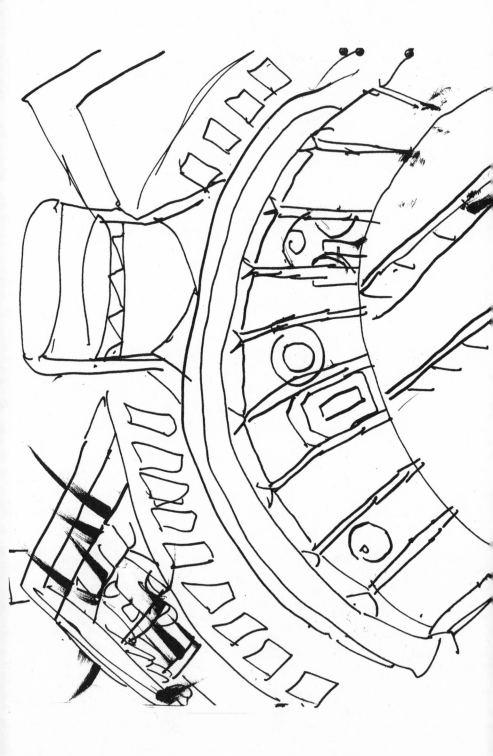

BARBER JUNCTION

SOUTHERN
SERVES
The SOUTH

CABOOSE CAR
Round house

KID DYNAMITE

Kid Dynamite was born on a papaya plantation, part Chinese, Indian, Greek, Irish and Polish and Jew—a mixture of many breeds. He did not wear his first pair of shoes until he reached his eleventh birthday; lived in the mountains in shacks, caves, huts, teepees, under trees and bridges; son of stars and moon, son of the Dingo dog and the ape and monkeys that roamed the forests and everglades and mountains of his native soil where he hunted for food, where he was cursed for this love of freedom and the music within him that made his face smile and eyes light up like the first western star in one twilight of his youthful years.

Kid came to America at the age of twelve. The Kid was sensitive and had a mighty right hand. He wept for the beauty of a flower and the beauty of Dingo dogs and kangaroos. He arrived in America on a tramp steamer. At Tacoma, Washington, he began washing dishes in a whorehouse; shined shoes, ran errands for alcohol and cigarettes; he would watch the lumberjacks get laid.

He did not like poor people pushed around. He did not like bosses or fear or shame. He did not like injustice or the crime of poverty. He did not like people crying over the price of meat. He did not like those who complained about Life.

He liked to hear Jazz and Honky Tonk. He liked the rags of Scott Joplin and the horn of Fats Navarro and Lester, and Bird, and Ella, and Sarah, Ma Rainey and Blue. He liked the Golden Sardine and the bass fiddle over the sky.

The Kid had a mighty right hand. The Kid liked jazz, and pussy and Zumi birds. He liked to take a leak in the streets —the yellow stream that flowed from within him—and look at the stars and the Moon and the Zodiac. He liked giant redwoods, and the eucalyptus trees in the Panhandle. Girls smiled at him and dogs and girls followed him in the streets. Every morning he woke up he wanted to die. He washed his face—wiping the devil and the dark thoughts from his mind.

At first light the Kid danced in the street, his eyes sparkled, the Kid had a mighty right hand.

The Kid was sensitive and pure as water; the Kid did not take shit. It was hard to take shit or take a good shit. His eyes were clear; his mind raced, like the clocks he wanted to stop. He liked bananas, and cherries; he liked potato pancakes and blondes. He broke a lumberjack's jaw who got too greedy with Annabelle in the whorehouse. It took one shot and it was all over. The Kid laughed at the moon, made love to Annabelle. The Kid had a mighty right hand.

The Kid went on the road and worked at different jobs; the Kid learned to cook and chop down trees; the Kid was five-foot-eleven; he was skinny and hard. The Kid could not take shit. He worked so well he frightened the other workers.

The Kid liked to drink apple juice for it was good for the soul. He liked to be kind to dogs and women. The Kid was a lover and he liked to be free—free as the wind and the stars, as the wild dogs he had seen in the gullies of Arizona and New Mexico: the skinny lean dogs that raced through the tumbleweed and the brush by the foot of the big mountains that crossed the continent.

The Kid read books about Indians, about brave Cochise, Sitting Bull, Hump, and the mighty Crazy Horse, about the brave Indians that once lived and roamed on the plains. He understood the spirit of fire and light and life.

The Kid roamed the mountains staying close to the dogs and the birds, staying close to the earth. He knew the warmth of fires and freezing cold of winters. The animals became his friends; the bird and the antelope; the rabbit and the running deer. The Kid had no desire to go back to civilization. The Kid had bright clear eyes that cut and sparkled like diamonds.

The Kid could not remember his mother or father. Only the rain of his childhood—the heavy rains of the Hawaiian Mountains. The papaya plantations were like slave camps.

All the young children worked in the hot sun; there was little time to play; and there was always fights, and ridicule and fear and death, and paranoia and MADNESS. There were tears of pain and exploitation; the boss was king and the foreman was the pimp of the kings; and the ignorant and the fearful worshipped the boss. The boss was cruel and vicious and the boss was king. The Kid had a mighty right hand.

The Kid became a prize fighter. He beat Joe Spud in Wala Wala—knockout, fourth round. Busted the poor guy's jaw. He beat Max Birch in three; Fat Cancer in seven; Benny Moose in nine; Whippet in twelve; Honkie Louie in six; knocked out Ali Baba in forty-one seconds of the first round; and decided to quit boxing because he did not like the face of the crowd. He did not like the pleasure of hate in the eyes of the multitudes.

The Kid went to take a walk in the forest and talk to the birds. The Kid had a mighty right hand.

The Kid roamed the earth. The trains and cars riding in the night; the cities and the small town alive with light and life. Texas, Montana, Nebraska, Idaho, Beaver Falls, Tucumcari, New Orleans, Boston, Rapid City, Goose Bay, Madison, Detroit, Apple Valley, New York, Tucson, San Diego, Chicago. San Francisco—city lights.

The Kid was the Polish prince of the wilderness. His long silver hair blowing in the distant breeze. The Kid kept moving on into the twilight.

Once the Kid ate watermelon and cried—it tasted too sweet. He talked to the stars and laughed at the moon. His Dingo dog, Submarine, was by his side. The Kid and Dingo moved on and out into the night. The Kid had a mighty right hand.

RACE OF THE CENTURY

1. DANNY BOY out~~BY~~ Kid Dreams & Subway Seren~
2. CHING'S Time ~~BY Manhattan~~ & String Bea~
3. Dreamy Kid BY HOT DOG & SHOE SHINE
4. SASS A FRASS BY Dreamers Wine & Roseland
5. ZODIAC BY SHOOT The MooN & LOST IN The Stre~
6. RACE The WIND BY MOON PRINCESS & Come AGAIN
7. CHINESE WAGON BY PICKPOCKET & American Dream
8. PURPle SAGE BY BlACK & Blue & Peeping Tom
9. ~~Dreamy Kid~~ Crippled Saint BY Shoes A Midget & Anky's AUNT
10. ~~Dreamy Kid~~ Brotherhood BY Lonely Kid & Book of Dream~
11. Rock of Ages BY Hurricane & Restless Wind
12. ~~Harolds Dream~~ Dream if Kings by Gospel Music & ~~Harolds Dream~~
13. ~~Dream of~~ Kings by Gospel Music & Hookers Bell
14. ~~Kid Universe~~. Harolds Dream by Stg Contass & Charing Prin~
15. River Wind by Indian Hemp & Take A CHA~
16. Artic Circle· by Liberty Bell & Ice Capade~
17. Kid Universe· by TACO MARY & Sunrise Sur~

ALSO ELIGIBLE   Crippled Saint
ERIN PRINCE   Brotherhood
Goldenrod   Rock of Ages
BAGS of Gold   HAROLD Dream
                       Dream of Kings
                       River Winds

Race of the Century

Irish Laughter By Kid Dreams & Subway Serenade
Madonna Princess By Short Skirt & Eyes of Green
Ching's Time By Madhatter & Stinging Bee
Dreamy Kid By Hot Dog & Shoe Shine
Erin Prince

Sassafras By Dreamers Wind & Roseland
Zodiac By Shoot the Moon & Lost in the Stars
Race the Wind By Moon Princess & Come Again
Chinese Wagon By Pickpocket & American Dreams
Kid Universe By Taco Mary & Sunrise Sam
Purple Sage By Black & Blue & Peeping Tom
River Wind By Gospel Music & Harold's Dreams
Crippled Saint By She's a Midget
Brotherhood By Lonely Kid & Book of Dreams
Rock of Ages By Hurricane & Restless Wind
Dream of Kings By Ice Capade & Money Tree

The City of Time

They race
Paradise
They scheme
They hustle
They Con
no magic but in nature
the trick baby of time
no magic in their eyes
time waits for no one
in time no one waits
those that wait
like slow trains
the air eats at them
the sky moves on
a baby carriage
the walk of shuffling feet
The Jew full of self consciousness
The bartender bored and restless
Time is like an incomplete pass
sailing alone in the end zone
The gorilla walks up and down in a cage
The convict
The secretary
The gallery owner his walls full of art
They all walk up and down
Like the going and coming to work
moving like the wind
anonymous and unknown
Like the seamen
The sailor
the wanderer
all on the same beat
across the seas of time
The eyes
The eyeless of a city
where the drummer beats wacking away
and the funky piano
moving to the fingers of Bert Bale
his horse laugh catching the latest rag

his eyes gleaming with the timeless lights of cities
each one on his own time
only the leopard springs
not the weary
or the poor
or the gutless in the gutters of time
lost queers
we are all queer
the grotesque of cities
the disenfranchised
the ones down with hate
the ones heavy with their victims
they too are eyeless
High in the Sierras
The eagle soars across the winter snow
across the peaks of east Utah
Colorado and California
The cities stand on the hill forever
it is quiet in the monasteries
nuns walk tip toe
no loud laughs there
nor sonic boom of planes
the women spurned and soiled with lost loves
the children doubting in the fairyland of playgrounds
warriors, clones are passing across boundaries
politicians heavy with sweat and lies and telephones
the infinite knowledge to know nothing   and sacks of mail
that each one
a shadow chases
a shadow hovers over them
a mother, a father, a grandfather, a loved one
a rare forgotten moment
for that is all there is forgotten moments
like memories
only the desperate knock
the landlord and the saints
not even Santa Claus knocks
the buses move on to Reno
the fifth race is on at Aqueduct
In California people move in large circles
criss crossing, double crossing
The Triple image of the Zulu's

A Harley Davidson races across the desert
The Forty Niners will lose again on a hail Mary pass
For only the freak will laugh last
The Time is his to move into the mainstream
To cover the void
To shake dispair
The tired children of time
The Indian General Hump rising out of a grave
Baudelaire to follow the red haired girl into a subway
Walt Whitman getting drunk on air
Charles Mills still writing symphonies in an Automat
Langston Hughes his sly grin greeting a hooker
Bodenheim writing another poem of wine
Mayakovsky walking across the Brooklyn Bridge
Steve Tropp on his knees at the Gaslight Café singing
hey Nunny, nunny, nunny, nunny forever
Janice Blue doing a cajun dance and indian polka
with Wayne Miller and Kell Robertson and Bernie a trio of time
Hey Bix, Hey Zoot, Hey Taj, Hey Van, Hey Joe, Hey You
Ring em Joe, I want them young
Coltrane, and Mingus and Philly Joe and Diz on the same set
Ask Bobby Jasper to play his flute
Bill Bosio his clarinet
and that stoned one armed cornet player
his right eye doing a solo forever

Crockett, California
Jan 5, 1984

A Look Back at My Youth

A highway crosses the playground of my childhood
the shoemaker is still on Archer Street
the druggist
the same faces inhabit the wilderness of the Bronx
its superstitions
its narrow minds
the synagogue
of old hebrews
the church of black cloth Catholics
its Irish sons with yellow ties
the football field is still there
night descends over the houses
Willy the mad Russian where are you
Tullo carrying ten men over the goal line
lost junky after the cheers died away
wild Murray where are you
Joey Cohen pimples on your face where are you
Little Abie do you laugh that loud anymore I wonder
voices of the children playing in the park
the boat house is deserted
the grass is still green in October
night is descending over the Bronx
the wilderness is but a memory
The Ritz movie is long gone
the whores have all moved away
It is time to go on
time moves so quickly
My mother still prays nightly
I used to play hooky and go to Bronx Park
and look at the lovers in the grass
the leaves are red and brown and green now
water flows down the falls of the Bronx River

Spring 1959

City at Dusk

In the wilds of Williamsburg
three boys play with toy guns
It is almost dusk
the boys shoot each other laughing
Smoke rises into the sky
The river weaves in mid-winter
some people laugh at midgets and cripples
and on the corner young punks look for fresh snatch
the legs of office girls and factory workers
their asses moving under iron girdles
Jews
Negroes
Puerto Ricans
living in the ghetto of a city
Cars race in all directions
Mrs. Simitz eats her borscht
It is four days old
there is rheumatism in the house
a pregnant girl
two cats
and a dog
named Charlie
the bridge is lit up with lights toward Manhattan
Olivia Sanchez
has a hard face
like the roar of trains
magnified with subway tokens
Manny scratches his behind
and the old Negro preacher buys some more cheap wine
glory is God's will
and he will never know
The sky is beautiful tonight
and most people hide behind walls weeping
A chazan chants a prayer
his brother Isaac got T.B.
and Nellie Hathaway needs ten bucks
she hustles for it
It is no crime this need of money
some people say that's what this world is all about

but who cares what people say
At dusk and the sky
These lights of the city
Drunk with darkness!

Brooklyn, New York
January 7, 1964

Poem Written in the Rain on Third Avenue

I'll send you a tulip
I'll give you a rose
love to children and peonies
So many beautiful girls in the city
These young fresh girls in the city
talking to their dogs and themselves
Nice doggie
Here doggie
they would say

O girls of the city
those thighs and belly laughing
Those eyes in the sky
laughing in the rain

Just lick a sweet nose
A dandelion thigh
sensuous leg
tongue
bright eyes like fishes
fingers like ballet dancers

Sweet buttery button in sunlight
pink lipped the slit
watery
the toes licking diamonds
her eyes in the sky

Sweet Rose and Lilac
Sweet Marge and Priscilla
Sweet Munch just a taste
O Shirley
I'll send you a tulip
I'll give you a rose

New York City
1973

excerpt from a letter to Bob Blossom

So I am born again
humble and lucky at that
It takes time to learn
faith lies inward
desire drives us mad
life leads us to the bar
or the empty street
hearing the voices of night
there is a bond that men have
It is sealed with life
our lives
our destinations
like the river
and so friend I say good night

It was a day

It was a day that reached almost to clouds
in the dark mine of reality that swallows me
in the streets of Sunday the jazz musicians stood
hawk eyed their voices strings
I tried to reach out to the nearest cloud
and only saw young girls who sang just words
their eyes like fairy tales
their noses trees
I could not reach the long paradise I yearn
maybe tomorrow I will find a ladder
and search within the sinew of my soul
this dark land I breathe the air of poetry
I cannot breathe no more
only stimulants to keep me going
in the streets of Sunday
I pray for rain to pour down and calm me

ROCK SONG

by Jack Micheline

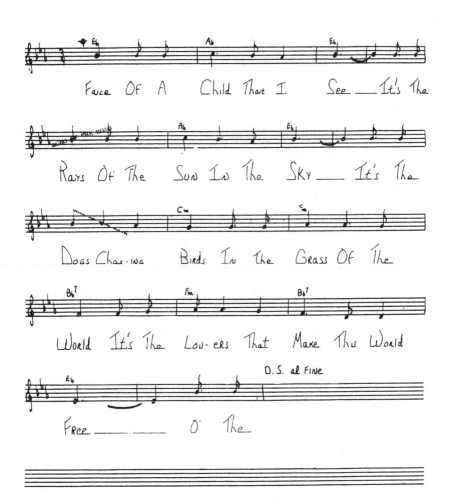

I stood
8 hours
in front of the church
        of Christ
    before I got a ride.

Your

Cunt

tastes

like

honey

Micheline 74'

THE CHICKENS AGAINST MAN

For over a hundred years chickens were raised for slaughter. Eggs were taken away from young mothers. Thousands of chickens were eaten at tables, at picnics, in homes all over the land.

The six hundred wild chickens who had escaped the pens in Petaluma roamed wild in the fields of California united in their revolt against man. Six hundred wild chickens planned their attack, choosing the fiercest chicken fighter of all, Red Neck, to lead them.

The chickens put sharpened steel points between the toes of their feet and wrapped them with silk string. The chickens under Gray Eagle, the old veteran flyer, took flying practice, learning to swoop down fiercely upon the enemy. Red neck chose Sunday Night in the first week of September to attack.

The pens of Petaluma lay in a huge valley surrounded by high mountains. Within these pens at Petaluma were two hundred thousand chickens, hens, roosters, and baby chicks.

The six hundred wild chickens became a disciplined, trained, united group who, for the first time in their lives, had a cause, a purpose, a belief to die for: to liberate all chickens enslaved by man, and eventually wipe man off the face of the earth. Blue Bonnett was chosen the ideological leader of the flock. His voice, reaching a dynamic crescendo, raised the morale and whipped hate into his forces.

The Sunday night in the first week of September came. Bright Crown, noted warrior of the wild birds and wildest fighter of the chickens, led the attack into the valley at the Pens of Petaluma. Wire clippers were especially made for the attack. Within twenty minutes twenty thousand chickens were free. Blue Bonnett was everywhere encouraging the chickens to fight more fiercely as Bright Crown and Red Neck led the attacks.

After a short fierce battle the Valley at Petaluma was liberated. And two hundred and twenty five chicken owners and their families were wiped off the face of the earth. The evacuation of two hundred thousand liberated chickens into the mountains was taking place.

The first battle against man was won.

Red Neck, Blue Bonnett and Bright Crown let their victorious and liberated Army across the mountains where they would continue their war against man.

1965

Hot Chicken Soup

Bernie walked all over town for special places
dairy restaurants, kosher restaurants,
inexpensive places, places with good soup and bread
places where he could eat a good meal

Bernie liked varnitchkes, kreplach, fruit salad
pumpernickel, sour rye, blintzes and cream
strawberries and hot chicken soup

When Bernie sat down to eat it was one of the
great acts of his life. His eyes lit up like a
pinball machine as he chewed, swallowed
and slurped his food down his bagpipe
Bernie walked five miles for a good hot bowl of soup
He was a prince
  a hawk,
    a wild bird
No one enjoyed a meal better than Bernie

San Francisco
January, 1975

Conversations On a Degenerate Street

Miss Babushka looked like a middle age housewife
She stood on the street in front of the art gallery
Her green blue eyes
I'm like a cat she said
Marie Babushka was not an ordinary hustler
Old German Freddy she met once a week
Clean used a rubber
Harry Katz the accountant wore boots and a black raincoat
Harry looked at her naked on the bed $17.50 a trick
Not bad for a few hours work
Miss Babushka had a great curved sense of humor
She laughed on the bed at the poor bastard
Time Square after Midnight priests were attracted to her
One cat from Monastery never came in his life
My child he said we are only human
I like to look at it he said to feel the skin of a woman
Free watches from a jeweler in Queens
Steak dinners from Freddy
Movies on Sunday Afternoon
Occasionally Miss Babushka went to Coney Island
I like the green stuff she said laughing
But I won't do the sixty nine
Looking for a free diaphragm the bitch was tight
Don't give any free stuff away bad for business
Took her for a coffee and a roll
She knew how to laugh Miss Babushka
A lot of men wanted to fuck her in the ass
I only got one hole and that's up front she said
She wasn't diversified enough no blow jobs
Just good American clean fun
Marie the cat had green and blue eyes
and she laughed like crazy
Long Live the Degenerates!

Death Orgy for the Lower East Side

Consuegua
High Yello
Hi Rummy
Gasoline
De Dungeons
Old Shuls
The Roaches
These Pigeons
Die Cellars
Old Skullcaps
The Rags of the Indians
Tomatoes
Potatoes
Alicante Ai Yay

O' Priest with a wishbone
O' Priest the lost junkies
used needles
old sticks for the fires
Consuegua
High Yellow
De Dungeons
No Pesos
Alicante Ai Yay

The stench of old mammals
the dance with a nose job
Barracuda
Ten sharks off Brooklyn
The freighters from Turkey
Bessarabian sailors
Polish Hunkies
Salami!
Cheese for the rabbits
Consuegua
High Yellow
De Dungeons
Alicante Ai Ay

Saturday Night
whiskey for dreamers
steps of the rumblers
The Screamers
O' Dreamers
Consuegua
High Yellow
De Dungeons
Alicante Ai Ay

Sunday, April 21, 1963

a beautiful old man
a cherubic spirit
a tired horse
a peddler with
dreams
an harmonica

THIS IS NOT A
COW THIS IS AN ANIMAL

NEW YORK

on every corner
There's a beggar
and a cripple
on every corner
There's a trashcan
on every corner There's
a dog on a leash
on every corner There's
a clown
on every corner
There's a child
on every corner
there's a star
and a dream

One night I saw Gandhi
kiss an old whore
while she lie drunk
in the bowery gutter
Walt Whitman came by
and kissed Gandhi
the old whore got up
on her feet singing

Oh God I feel so blue
Oh God I feel so blue

I want to open up my eyes an cry
I want to open up my eyes an die

I want to open what's under my eyes
and feed it to the two faced Christ

angels under my skin
angels under my skin

wanna paint Christ blue
wanna paint Christ blue

Oh God I feel so blue
Oh God I feel so blue

Blues

I'm on the road
I'm on the stone

that's all loves me
Is dogs and little children

I'm on the road
I'm on the stone

that's all loves me
Is dogs and little children

SONG of Kid Wonder

1. Dupity Doo
4. Dupity DA
9. Dupity Loo
9. Dupity Doo

3. Hey Loo
5. Hey Hoo
8. Hey Coo Loo
8. Hey Coo Loo

6. Hey Joo
6. Hey Loo
6. Hey Coo
6. Hey Soo

Doo DA
Ding Tune Hey Soo

2. Bo Dee
2. Bo Hee
2. Bo See

7. Dinga Jing Hey Hoo
4. Dinga Bins Hey Loo
6. Dingc Ming Hey Soo

6. Ding DA Sing Hey Joo

10. Dupity Hoo Hoo Loo — Loo — Loo — Yo! Yo! Yo! Yo!
Dupity Hoo Loo Yo! Yo! Yo! Yo! Yo!

the guys are rare birdes
Rare birdes fly in the edges of the sky
they only come out
when the other people are asleep.

In Central Park On Yom Yipper
Meeting Joseph Delaney Over A Cup of Coffee
Remembering his Brother Buford and a St. In Paris

Holy Men
On Holy Days
An Old Man
Kind Eyes
A Sad Face
The Hard Solitary Life
of painters in America
The Bear
The Lion
The Jackal
The Monkeys
You Got Some Brother Joe
Some Brother
Holy Man
Gandhi
Mary Painter
Jimmy Baldwin
Lucien
The Nut House
Chatterton
To Give totally in the darkness
The Neon Lights
Barbazol
The Coupe
Martin Engleman
John Graham
Houdini
The Magician
Who will know
This Mad Freak
This cat with a brush
Buford Delaney
The Holy Man with a glow in his eyes
Ain't no road he's been on
Just an ordinary journey
Just being himself
In a working Class section
In a small street in Paris

A raggedy Ass painter
A million paintings in a closet
Vegetables to share
Dinner with a mad poet
Love is cruel, Life is cruel
walking Paris
in the arms of a man
who knows the elegance of the sun
his eyes rotating flowers
 I Love
 The Lost Sky
 On some Forgotten ▬▬▬
 My song of truth and Fire
 horses flying in the sky
 flying horses in the stars
 Redbirds singing fly away
I sought sorrow in a city
The dark friends for a moment
Takes you through fire
and the dark night
and I laugh Rainbows
Sing me a song Moma
Sing it nice and sweet
Sing it Moma
With a Beat
Sing it High
and sing it Sweet
Sing it Moma
With a Beat!

New York City
July 1970

Sunshine Hotel

There's The Sunshine Hotel
There's The Sun up in the Sky
There's Freedom being born
And Freedom when we die

There's Big Dipper George
And NewBerry Slim
Miss Lemon Bocay
And Happy Miss Grim

There's The Sunshine Hotel
There's The Sun up in the sky
There's Freedom Being Born
And Freedom when We Die

Not Far From The Yard Is Strawberry Hill
There's African Pete
and Bettle Mouth George
Crazy Willy on Drums
ShoeShone on The Moon

And After They Jam
They go to their Rooms
Get High and Make Love
In The Sunshine Hotel
There's The Shine Hotel
There's The Sun Up In The Sky
There's Freedom Being Born
And Freedom When We Die

There's Big Dipper George
And NewBerry Slim
Miss Lemon Bocay
And Happy Miss Grim

There's The Sunshine Hotel
There's The Sun up in the sky
There's Freedom Being Born
And Freedom when we die

My Mother was a
humble and kind lady
who loved God
and me very much.
She thought I wrote dirty stories

Jack Micheline

WALKING ON
WATER WASN'T
BUILT IN A DAY

They Took The sky FROM Thier eyes
They Took The sun FROM Thier hair
They Took The Moon FROM Thier Nose
They Took The ring FROM Thier shoes
They took The sound FROM Thier brow
A leaf FROM Thier heart
And Took The ANIMAL AWAY
And Left The shell ON The ground
That passed away

white haze of the forest breaking
Through

They took The sound from Thier bro
They Took A leaf from Thier heart
They took The ANIMAL away
And put em in a cage
And left The shell on The ground
That passed Away

white haze of The forest breaking
Red comets roaring over through
white haze of The forest breaking thru

Carl's song

Come on MomaMMove on Moma Lets Go
Come on Popa Move on Popa Lets Go
Come on KinderxxxxxxGo
Come on Doggie XXXXX
                                    Lets Go

    Shake it Moma
    Shake it Popa
    Shake it Kinder
    Shake it Susie
    Shake it ANNIE
    Shake it Moma

Come on Susie Shake it Moma Lets Go
Come on Annie Shake it Moma Lets Go
 Come on Doggie Shake It MomA Lets Go

 Come on Moma Move it Moma
 Come on Popa Shake It Popa
 Come on Moma Shake it Popa

   Come on Jack Shake It Jack

  Shake it Moma Shake it Moma

 Move it in and move it out
   Shake it
 Shake it Annie
  Shake it Susie
   Shake it Kinder

  Move it in and Move it out
   Lets go Moma Shake it Moma
   Move it in and move it out
    Shake it Moma
    Shake it Popa
    Shake it Kinder
    Shake it Susie
    Shake it Annie
    Come on Jack and Shake it Moma
   Move it Popa
   Shake it Moma
    Move it Kinder
    Shake it Doggie

      Come on Moma
       Move it Moma
        Shake it Popa
       in and out
         Shake it Moma
          Shake it Moma

Muscatel

Ya
know mister
Da
    worlds
           not
               here.
I
    tell
       ya
         I
             see
                gorillas.
It
    really
         never
             rained
                 yet.
whens tomorrow ,
the dog eats fish
da moon never lied
people they someplace else
the birds have wings

we is all winners
but we all lose
      I
      tell
      you
      I
      see
      G
       O
        R
         I
          L
           L
            A
             S
     yeah
     gorillas.

ALL THOSE LOSING
HORSES IN THE STRETCH
AT SANTA ANITA AQUEDUCT
GOLDEN GATE, Belmont, Hollywood Par

SMILE AT THE BIRDIE

Dixie hustled on the boulevard each night avoiding black
and white dicks, trying to raise money to get back to Ken-
tucky. The Freaks come out from everywhere. They come
out like roaches into the dark night, from side streets and
back alleys, from cheap hotels and rooming houses, from
apartments and fancy homes and ranches in the valleys and
canyons. The misfits and misplaced of the planet earth.

All streets lead to the great white way, Hollywood Bou-
levard. America's fantasyland, like the pinball machines that
glare in colored lights onto the cement and stardust. Nothing
is real but the twenty dollars handed a hooker for her trick.
Tricks are real and even the mannequins in the store win-
dows look real. The magic formula of stardust and dreams
and a little perfume, sexy underwear and hot eyes and
lipstick and the glare of neon and tinsel. The music grinding
out from sound studios which dot the town like a speckled
bird. The great white way extends from Vine to La Brea.

Dixie was accosted by young black toughs out of Watts
who paraded their new macho, inspired by T.V. and the new
black movies. Only a century before there were only 75
ranches occupying the valley. Way before Griffith and Chap-
lin and Valentino and Garbo and then came the talkies, the
modern pictures and Dylan and the Beatles. It was all hot,
arid, lazy desert.

The crash of '29 and the Okies crossed the desert and
then came Bette Davis and Bogart and John Garfield. Mari-
lyn Monroe's pretty face lies under the Hollywood earth.
With the movie stars came the gangsters, the lawyers, the
pimps, the agents and the solicitors and the huge movie lots
and film studios. Hollywood became America's number one
meat grinder as a century before Chicago was the meat-
packer of the world.

Hollywood was the builder of stars not to mention the
bronze stars which dot the sidewalks, up Hollywood Blvd.
and down Vine St. in between Thrifty's and Swenson's and
Frederick's and Grauman's Chinese Theatre.

The L.A. valleys and canyons are inhabited by millions
of people. Men and women and children coming with dreams

from all over America. A grand ménage, as Adolf Menjou would say. Everything's on a grand scale in Los Angeles County where there are more cars than cockroaches.

In Downtown L.A. below Hill and Spring lies the biggest skidrow in America. The rummies. The wasted from the wars. The mentally crippled. The alcoholics. The ones who didn't play the game. The derelicts over a fire in vacant lots heating sterno and wood alcohol. The ones who fought alone and fell down from exhaustion. The compassionate with too much heart. The beaten and the freaks and the crazies and the lost and the damned, thousands spread out among the cheap hotels and flophouses. And the only natural thing that blossomed in the desert was the Cactus.

Chooko was a Queen and she walked the streets. She was sixteen and she was tall and skinny and had beautiful eyes. Her beautiful red wig. Her succulent lips.

It was Friday night and people were lining up in front of Figaro's on Melrose. At Rupert's bodies weaved in and out, dancing to the music of the disco. Music blared into the street. On La Cienega Blvd. a rich woman artist set up her own art opening. Her paintings reflected the bored faces of the diamond-studded ladies wrapped in furs on a summer's night. The champagne glasses clinked in their hands and up the street on Santa Monica Paul the truck driver was still writing hillbilly songs at Barney's Beanery.

Limousines, Fiats, Camaros and Commodores. Long, hot, flashy cars cruised up and down the street like a merry-go-round. Five thousand cars heading for the great white way. Some going to fashionable restaurants and chop houses. People and cars just coming and going like revolving doors. The great white sign hovering over the city called Hollywood. The voice of Billy Eckstein from the radio on the Capitol Tower. His son, Matthew, walking mumbling writing poems in the streets of New York.

On the hot summer days the bodies line up on the beaches looking for a suntan. Thousands of cars roam the streets and thousands of faces walk up and down the beaches. Thousands of dreams and fantasies. Welcome to Fantasyland. Hollywood the builder of images. The builder of stars.

Chooko walks up and down the streets smiling, talking to himself: "Hey, Sweetie pie," he says, laughing in the night. Riding the 85 bus going downtown on Wilshire Blvd., a cute blonde gives me the eye. She sits down next to me and the back of her shirt reads "New Jersey".

"You from New Jersey, baby?" I say.

She is built better than a fancy automobile. She smiles and traces her life for me: New Jersey, Florida, Colorado and California. She wants to live in Hermosa Beach. Her name is Joyce. Her eyes like pure blue crystal. I get a hard-on just looking at her. Joyce gets off the bus too quickly for me to ask her for her phone number.

Ben Chauncey works as a scout for one of the record companies. He holds auditions for new talent down in his basement in West Hollywood, taping the new sounds of young aspiring musicians and singers that come into the city from across the nation.

Ben knows how to smile at the birdie. (In Chicago there are a hundred ways to sell the bull after it's slaughtered.) The record industry is as cut-throat as the Chicago slaughter houses. Cutting, selling and distributing one hundred different parts of the meat.

At the Cinco de Mayo parade the politicians smile and wave their hands at the crowds and they too know how to smile at the birdie. Rarely ever walking down skidrow. Denying it exists. The dehumanization of man. The cheers rise up from Dodger Stadium and the Los Angeles Coliseum: "Hit 'em again harder! Win! Shout! Holler! Shout! Stay ahead of the pack! You got to be number one, you got to stay on top." All the pain in the world tied up in knots, ready to explode like a time bomb.

The birds sing in the morning. At night lions and snakes roam the streets. Sharpies with white Cadillacs. In the suburban ghettos the rats and roaches crawl. In a small room the Camptown Races plays on the radio. Every weekend thousands of cars go up and down the boulevards. A misplaced city of freaks and misfits.

People looking, people starving for culture, people wanting to touch, to feel, to be human. People dreaming. The California dreamers all around. The voice of Jose Feliciano on the radio.

The freaks come from everywhere. They come out like roaches into the dark night or into the sunlight. From

cheap hotels and rooming houses. From side alleys and back
streets. The parade is on Hollywood Blvd. The hustlers,
the pimps, the thieves, the tourists from Europe and South
America and the Orient. They come out of nowhere into the
concrete, stone and glitter. Out of the glare of the sun and
the stars.

Dixie walks the streets saying, "You want any pussy,
baby?" Dreaming of her Kentucky home. I remember the
blonde getting off the bus. What eyes! Her rhythm and
smile! It's the people that count. The one lone, solitary,
smiling bird.

Hollywood!
Long live People!
Viva Feliciano!
Viva the Universe!

Santa Monica, California
July 16, 1978

Poem for St. Terresa and the World

LET'S GO TO THE MOVIES
LET'S GO FOR A DRIVE
NO TIGHT PANTS
JUST A SHORT SKIRT
NO PANTIES ON
JUST YOU AND ME
HARD COCK
LONG TONGUE
AND YOUR OPEN THIGHS
IN THE RAIN
UNDER THE STARS
OPEN THE ROOF OF THE SKY
LET THE FANTASY DIE
LET THE DREAM COME ALIVE
LET THE JUICES FLOW
LET THE LITTLE BIRDY SING
LET IT ALL HANG OUT
LAUGHING OUR BALLS OFF
LET'S ALL GET IT ON
LET'S ALL BE HAPPY
LET ALL THE WORLD SING
A COCK AND PUSSY SONG

San Francisco
July 29, 1995

An Ant in My Shoe

Across the floor
an ant crawls
into my shoe
It is after midnight
I will go out and walk
the Tenderloin streets till dawn
the pain in my groin operation
lingers on like a decayed tooth
Where are the noble ones?
I see your faces each night
a flashback to my bohemian past
Charles Mills on a park bench in Sheridan Square
All walking with me in a great dream above the stars
Mingus on bass at the Five Spot
Franz Kline on a bar stool at the Cedar Bar
his sad face and eyes of disbelief
Kerouac in a daze walking across America
in his great American dream
Freddy Redd and Cecil Taylor doing a duet on Ninth street
Freddy Mogubgub and Mario Jorrin together laughing
Tom Halley the wino on a bench in Washington Square
All walking with me in a great dream above the stars
the poor Jewish poet and singer Harold Goldfinger
still keeps that dream alive at the Albert Hotel
I keep on walking in a great dream above the stars
Pete the Greek is doing breakfast at Tina's
the soft gentle eye of Milly serving the breakfast
waiting on the morning tables
Monaco the Barber on Golden Gate five foot two
a humble smile who digs God and old time music
Isaac the scholar in a bookstore on Turk Street quiet and
        gentle
I hear Kell Robertson singing again
across the Mission at the Ribeltad
Bernie Uronovitz still playing Frisbee
and Tom Keats smiling on his old guitar
in a bistro on Colombus Avenue

Bob Kaufman smiling covering my tired body
in the Western Addition
Maybe only a Mad Jew or a Mexican
          or a lost Indian
          or an unknown poet
          or a waitress who has eyes
          or a redhead on a bus
          or a horse that sweeps the field
A hooker stands alone on a street corner all night long
Some skinny old man on a rainy night with one tooth
playing a harmonica against the walls of time
The sky is above us
maybe it is the eyes of knowing the light that is too bright
that leaves us limp and haggard
Pity those that look the other way this is most of us
this world is hard and sad indeed
fear and greed turn the wheels of time and nations
These significant souls their eyes speak to me
Their eyes that speak make the stars shine brighter
their gifts of kindness are significant deeds
the acts of plain people
simple souls are shooting stars that curve into the night sky
It is difficult to go to public places
I am already too infamous
like a rare bird and freak of nature
who carries treasures of the mind to each watering hole
across the great American desert
some Paparazzi will shove a camera in my face
to capture a fading image of a bent and tired soul
trying to tie a shoelace weaving in the winds of time
It is a sad world when one loses the light
The Ant is crawling in my shoe on a wooden floor
It will be a long painful night again
What I really want to do is go mad on a canvas
to go crazy on paper
to take the colors of all the rainbows
using hand and brush spit and sweat and balls
and every tissue of my mind that flies into unknown worlds
to kick the crud and fear of decay and decadence
push and smash and cum into spurting seed that conquers

death
It is a long and painful night again
The memory of my Mother walking off a hotel roof into
    oblivion
You can count the people you really love on two fingers
Record your highest moments in a tiny little book
An Ant is crawling in my shoe
Lift up that cup again brother show me the way to go home

Bakery Café,
San Francisco
August 7, 1988

Appendix

Imaginary Interview with Jack Micheline
by Jack Micheline

What do you think poetry is?

I don't know what it is. What I do know the word must have
its own music. It must jump off the page. Because one writes
poetry it doesn't make one a poet. What person in his right
mind would be a poet anyway? It's a rare spiritual gift given
by the gods to a few souls.

What poets influenced you—?

Federico Garcia Lorca's "Poet in New York"
Sherwood Anderson's MidWestern Chants
Maxwell Bodenheim's "Beyond Irony"
Whitman's "Leaves of Grass"
Charles Baudelaire's "Flowers of Evil"
Allen Ginsberg's "Kaddish"
Vachel Lindsay songs
also "The Spoon River Anthology" by Edgar Lee Masters.
Rimbaud, Mayakovsky, Some turk I don't remember his
name. The magnificent wonder of Jack Kerouac his life influ-
enced me. As did Charlie Mingus, Franz Kline. Mario Jorrin
a rare photographer in the 50s and 60s

More or less Life influenced me. Anyone real and aware
influenced me, since I never wanted to be poet. I thought all
poets were sissies. And I became one. Life is full of Irony.
Life is full of hard knocks ups and downs. When I left the
Sweater factory in the garment center to go out to climb the
mountain of truth, and I attempted to capture the cities with
my pen and pencil I mean. That in itself was a hell of a rea-
son to be alive. To Capture New York, Chicago, New Orleans
Los Angeles and San Francisco. To walk the streets of my
land out of my mind. It was the highest religious experience
I ever had.

One morning in the streets of South Brooklyn, Antonio
Machado, Bowler Hat and cane, lifted his hat to me and
smiled in the early morning. Lorca speaks of the Duende

the Spirit he writes when one is walking in the open air. He speaks of the pencil moving on the pages automatically. There is a muse and many Gods and there are angels flying up, there in the sky. It takes so much strength to be real to go out of one's skin. To be a real poet.

What advice would you give to a young poet today?

Stay away from poetry schools. Or groups. Stay away from power freaks. Go to the people they are the fertilizer of your poems. Send your poems out to friends send them out to strangers. Read and sing in strange bars in restaurants, in parks, discover America again. America has never been discovered. It has been seduced.

I don't write too much anymore. Only when I'm moved. There are a lot of good poets around and a few great ones. Bukowski wrote some good earlier work. But he has fell on his ass. He drank from the bottle of fame and it sucked his juice.

I have a number of manuscripts that have never been published, "The Notes Of The Lost Cities" a journal I kept when I walked through the cities in the late Fifties and Early Sixties, a very important work where the Duende is actually described. The Love poem that reaches high above the cities.

The most important thing that ever happened to me was meeting "Ed Balchowsky" artist one-armed veteran of the Lincoln Brigade. Whose eyes shone so bright, Whose heart was as big as Russia. His Buddy Ken Krebs also influenced as well as his brother Harold and dead mother Jenny. I met these people in Chicago in the streets and lofts and rooftops of a city. These guys never gave up. They're growing sunflowers now.

It's all got to do with the light. Walking at dusk as the light turns you can feel the world turn with you, when I was younger the cities turned me on the dog wags its tail

Fuck the Business of Poetry, make love some where. The way a shoemaker hammers a nail could be the greatest poem of all. How do dead people write poems or teach writing? You got to be alive inside. You got to have juice. You got to learn to sing your own song. You got to sing it loud and clear. You can't be afraid to be yourself. To find your sound. Go out into the unknown find your muse the gods are still there, walk out into the night and dance and talk to the moon. Then you can smile at me as if you didn't know it already.

Berkeley, CA
August 23, 1982

THE PROMISE OF AMERICA

THEY HAVE TAKEN

AWAKE
THE
DEAD
FROM
THERE
LUMBER
MAN
IS
NOT
A
BIRD
HE
IS
AN
ASSHOLE

THE
PROMISE
OF
AMERICA
AND
PROSTITUTED
IT
ALL
FOR
MONEY
AND
POWER
IF
ART
IS
FOR EVERYBODY
WHY NOT GIVE IT AWAY

THEY
HAVE
BURIED
THE
FLOWER
OF
THIS
NATION

THERE
IS
SO
MUCH
SILENCE
HERE
IT
IS
NOT
FUNNY
ANYMORE

I WANT TO THANK THE FOLLOWING PERSONS
WHO PASSED THROUGH MY LIFE
WHEN I FIRST MOVED TO THE VILLAGE IN 1955
AND ALSO THE PERSONS, PEOPLE AND SOULS
WHO I LATER MET ON MY TRAVELS TO THE WEST COAST
THE TIME SPANS TWENTY SEVEN YEARS
IF SOME ARE LEFT OUT IT IS DUE TO LAPSE OF MEMORY
PLEASE FORGIVE ME

Tom Halley, Robert Blossom, Warren Finnerty, Mario
Jorrin, Harold Goldfinger, Franz Kline, Marty Pajeck,
D'Hirsh Margolin, Harold Anton, Malcolm Rapheal, Izzy
Young, Jamie Perpinyan, Richard Pepetone, Diane DiPrima,
Kirby Doyle, Jack Kerouac, Charlie Mingus, Brooker Irwin,
Curtis Porter (Shafi Hadi), Bob Feldman, Skinny Louie,
Marvin Miesel, Noel Jutte, John Krushnick, Jean Cohen,
Miriam Redding, James Baldwin, Jimmy the Greek, Tommy
Trantino, James T. Farrell, Henry Miller, Sue Kulby, Alix
Geluardi, Street Walkers, Ira Cohen, Night Prowlers,
Martin Kerns, dreamers, visionaries, saints, rummies, old
Bohemians, Pepper Adams, James Mitchell, John Mitchell,
Dave McSeehy, Johny Romero, Zoot Sims, Cecil Taylor,
Freddy Red, Jackie McLean, Steve Tropp, Howard Hart,
Bob Bolen, Francis Carlyle, The Dutchess, White Crombie,
Foxy Lewis, Fat Black Pussy Cat, San Remo, Ray Freed,
Louie's Tavern, Bleeker Tavern, Kettle of Fish, Pandoras
Box, Robert Claremont, Danny Maltese, Jake Spenser,
MacTavish, Brigit Monahan, Stanley Gould, Herbert
Huncke, Indian Willy, Dutch, Loka Ralley, Gaton, Gasten,
Jim Kolb, Bill Heine, Janine Pommy Vega, Fernando Vega,
Maxwell Bodenheim, Beauford Delaney, Ray Parker, Tony
Bender, Cedar Tavern, Herman Cherry, Mike Donahue,
Jacimian Proubst, Ronnie Madiglianico, Maurice, Crazy
Ira, Raymond Howell, cat ladies, bag ladies,Kaldns, Dylan
Thomas, Gregory Corso, Big Brown Kiwi Bar, Lenny
Horowitz, Ricky Sanchez, Big George the sculpture, Stanley
Postak, Jane N, Crazy Jake, Charlie O, Irene Cavendish,
Indian Jim, Fugazi Bar, Philip Lamantia, Blossom Dearie,
Bobby Jaspar, John Krushnick, Shel Silverstein, Cafe
Figaro, Rosemarie, Jim Knighton, Julie K, Risa Korson, The
ghost of Sixth Avenue, Goddy's bar, Annie, Trixall Wheeler,
Jazz on the Wagon, Leroi Jones, Romany Marie, Charlie

Stark, Kim Hall, Jimmy Atkins, Denny Richmond, Jimmy
Cuchiara, Casy Lee, Robert Cordier, Al Delauro, Ginger
McCormick, Nancy Gilbreath, Lonnie Elder the 2nd, Will
Guy, Red Fred, Susan Catherine, Lucy, Paddy O'Sullivan,
Tuil Kupferberg, Jimmy the racetrack Lyons, Rosalie
Sorrels, John Cohen, Gerry Mulligan, Dave Van Ronk, Mike
Fannelli, Jesses Quillians, Hubert Selby Jr., The Fifty Five
Bar, The naked Ladies on the Island of Manhattan, Harlem,
Langston Hughes, Dave Henderson, Lenox Avenue, Central
Park, The Christopher Street Pier, The Lower East Side,
Bill Saroyan, Delancey Street, MacDougal Street, Odetta,
Johnny Baker, Cowboy, The Girls from Brooklyn, Red
Grooms, Bob Thompson, Paul Krassner, Lester Johnson,
Ornette Coleman, Charlie Parker, Richard Bright, Charles
Mills, Indian Willy, Dave Milton, John Coltrane, Robert
Frank, Dody Muller, Miles Forst, Barbara Forst, Walking in
the night on the Bowery, West Fourth Street across town,
Jim Davis, Arnie Nelson and Family, Herb Poyta, Ronaldo
Burnet, Tom Hall, S. Clay Wilson, John Bellah, Dave
Gieser, Charles Wehenberg, Charles Glasser, Sally John
Bryan, Elinor, Steven Kush, Paul Kelly, Peter Pussydog,
Dierdra Evans, The guys on the rail at Bay Meadows and
Golden Gate Park, Jenny, Muldoon Elder, Doug Moody,
Kave McDonaugh, David Plumb, Trieste Cafe, New York
Jack, Society Jack, Rich Paulley, Sam Dietch, Ed Moose,
Warren Hinckle, Some Genius screaming on a mountain
Top, The Mother of Charity, John Geluardi, Vincent Silver,
Helen Silver, Socrates, Steve Schenk, Floyd Salas, Tony,
Tom and Johnny of the DeSoto Cab Company, Carl Solomon,
Robert Valenza, Andy Clausen, Michael Wochuczk, F.A.
Nettlebach, Pam Beran, The Bubble Gum Lady on Telegraph
Avenue, Brooklyn Heights, Lola Wolfe, Michael Walter,
Jane Fiago, Allen Ginsberg, Bill Burroughs, Ilke Soobie,
Guareholtz of Indiana, Zelda Balchowsky, Ed Balchowsky,
Ken Krebs, Ira Nowinski, Josie Grant, Ron Turner, John
Norton, Alda Humes, Ken Kesey, Babs, Waco, Joe, Willy
across America, Publisher of Willy Magazine, Buk, One ball
Louie, Ann Weldon, Thomashevsky of Oregon, Norweigian
Bob, Bob Miller, Bobby Donlin, Bernie Uroovitz, Lawrence,
Thomasina Demaio, Kristie Stiles, Mark Hasenkamp,
Country Joe, Wavy Gravy, Taj Mahal, Judy Foster, Kell
Robertson, Kirk Robertson, The Freak of Santa Monica

Blvd., Peter Dean, Rayford Liles, Jean Cohen, Indian Willy,
Southampton Max, Puffy's Bar, Stanley of West Broadway,
Street Painters of New York, Shoe Shine Joe, A.D. Winans,
Riverboat Sam, Marketta, Phil Kelly, Mexico City Blues,
Philliphion Bob, The Living Theatre, The Magic Theatre,
Alvin of Cafe Babar, Q.R. Hand, The Lost Arab of Esclaon,
Josephine Petrone, Johnny Antonelli, Billy Zionist, Willy,
May, Aunt Rose and my brother Eddie and to my son
Vincent Silver riding in the Arizon night, VIVA Creation—
Ai Ay.

13 February 1983
Denver, Colorado

Letter to Kerouac in Heaven   Globesville, Colo
                                     Oct 15, 1984
                                     4411 Logan
                                     Denver Colo 80216

Dear Jack,

I'm sorry I've never made it, but I tried to do it my way.
I just could not find a courageous publisher with distribution.
None of my 9 books can be found in any American bookstore.
I want to thank you for your encouragement. It's been a
long hard road. Bobby Miller is still getting drunk in North
Beach on week-ends. He tells some good corny jokes he must
be close to sixty and he still chases girls—Goldfinger is still
alive in the Village. Walking the streets, that beautiful crazy
Jewish elevator man. Harold Anton has passed and your
drinking buddy the composer Chuck Mills has departed the
earthly plane. They had a Kerouac Conference at Boulder a
couple of years ago. You would have been proud of me. Ken
Kesey gave me the most valuable performance award. A
bottle of wine for Harvey Silver, and a bottle of whiskey for
Jack Micheline.[1] I was really on that afternoon and I hope
you heard me up there in Heaven. I hear Bobby Donlin is
still alive managing some club in Cambridge. Charlie Min-
gus is also gone, passed away. gave up the ghost. People are
more frightened than ever now. The reason I never made it.
I wouldn't <u>play</u> the <u>game</u> or <u>ball</u> with the publishers, they
seem so self-involved, publishing mediocrity. <u>Rick Kids</u> play-
ing games with a pack of ass kisses always around them,
when was it any different. The <u>arts</u> is not for us poor kids.
we create because we have no choice. It is what we have
to do—no matter what. I swear I am not jealous of these
people. with their power that is the way they show their
love. I guess I should have more compassion, they always
refuse to go for a walk in the sunlight. <u>Frightened Men</u>. The
Ring of fear. Sing me a song baby Blue. A song that rises to
the heavens. A song that dances with The Stars .. Sing me a
song Baby Blue. A song of the open road. You have a beauti-
ful daughter, Jack. By the name of Jan. I don't see much of
Allen and Peter. I was never close to them, they seem cold

---

[1] Jack Micheline was born Harold Silver, also known as Harvey Martin
Silver, on November 26, 1929 in the Bronx, New York City.

and detached, they're lousy trying to make it. But you see I always was a loner, A bare stick in the water, A hot piece, An outlaw, A runner, Doing my chaotic happy dance across this land. I want to tell you, I tried Baby. God knows how I tried to say it like it never was said before.

You know this world never loved genius, we exist in spite of the world. I heard Charles Mills talking to the lions once in Central Park. He wrote over 90 pieces of music in his lifetime. I'm putting this book together—Let's Ride the angel goodbye! I am staying with an old buddy from Chicago now in Denver named Ken Krebs, you'll be happy to know all your work has taken off all over the world. They read you everywhere now. You are a departed legend of time, and I guess you knew it all the time. I saw Carl Solomon at the Kerouac Conference. He still lives with his mother and works as a messenger boy. I was in TAOS New Mexico last [break in manuscript] celebrating an art show at Shadoni of Bill Gertz a painter friend. A guy you would have loved to have known. He introduced me to Geronimo's grandson who is a painter and a poet. Heavy dude you take one look at him. He gives you the willies he is <u>so real</u>. Life goes on to the end. I hope they are treating you nice in heaven. You know how it was on the earth and I hope it's better up there.

Love your friend,
Jack Micheline

P.S. your acquaintance Rainy Cass disappeared, The guy, The sleepwalker from New Orleans, The guy who plays the cornet and put out Climax magazine. Some guy named Willie put out a magazine called The Willie, he disappeared too. It seems all the good people disappear. There are too many phoneys in the world. The arts are loaded with them. Somehow <u>we must rescue the consciousness of man</u>. Some way some noble purpose must exist. Away to a new <u>aware-ness</u>. At the Kerouac Conference Chellon Holmes was such a Beautiful gentleman. He really loved you Jack. He called you <u>the great rememberer</u> and read a soulstirring piece about you, what rare, fine soul. and such a gentle spirit. Too many people do not live their poems. We are still in the dark ages baby. Bless you Jack your kind gentle spirit. Shig is still alive and is very sick and has moved to Southern California to spend his last years. The one armed *[words missing in manuscript]*

I hope you are well in heaven. And god bless the damned and bless the angels too. bless em all the long and the short and the tall, bless all their children and their bastard sons Bless em all.

Remember that song Jack
Bless Em All!

Love
forever
Jack Micheline

I'm looking out the window of my favorite
bar called the Uptown Bar. Some mad, poor, young hooker
is walking barefoot in a cold night. Some poor fucking mas-
ochist, money won't help her. Not the fleeting companion-
ship for 15 minutes a trick for $75. That won't ever help the
poor soul. Life is cruel. The Real is too Real for most people.
One cannot be a teacher. Each one must go through the fire.
SURVIVE or DIE. Grow or Die. It is not easy for me com-
ing back to SF. I've never been recognized here nor do I seek
recognition from the Established Order. I'm not a big time
person. Maybe a class in my resume. I've been on The Front
Lines too damn long, Sweetheart. I'm tired Sweetheart,
very tired. I feel like a character from one of my songs.
ONE cannot transmit Freedom-openness AWARENESS to
another Being. Impossible! Not even the wildest dreams can
you rub off on someone else. We're living in an impossible
dream. But with all doubt and momentary flashes of wisdom.
1995 is going to be my year. Yes indeed, 1995, Whippee!

I am mailing back your Zippy. I've redeemed it for I am the
REDEEMER. THE GREAT REDEEMER to RESUR-
RECT THE OLD THE USED THE DECAYED. To give
new life to what has already fallen into the aches and dung
heaps of time. No one really knows who I am. What I've
tried to do. Great Gurus, teachers, work in small ways. That
is why TV Sucks and most establishment sucks. It is all be-
side the point. The basic premise is I propose a real deep and
meaningful friendship with you.

Amelia, you have given too many free shows to the masses.
You are too rare, too talented, too unique to continue your
mad dance inside. I want you to retain your uniqueness.
Your rare and magnificent gifts. Indeed we've always lived
in the dark ages. For those who have been on the mountain.
And we have been both on the mountain together. I have
lived in voluntary poverty all my life. I have never been
involved with The Establishment. I dislike everything they
represent. Like you I DO MY OWN THING. And every-
thing I do or create I try to be original. I always seek new
ways, new songs, new interpretations. My spelling is atro-

cious. Forgive me, my tongue will always be where you so
desire it. My dearest animal and friend Amelia, with eyes of
husky dogs.

Keep this date open. FEB 14. Coppola's party for Inglenook
Winery. I am planning something wild, something spec-
tacular. MY ALASKAN DINGO. MY BINGO BABY. MY
DOLL. I am planning a wild scene in northern California.
For you Amelia. An impromptu spur of the moment dance
and song. At a monied party. An establishment of the Spring
Season. I want people to see you in all your GLORY. I want
to blow the establishment up. Blow their middle class asses
off this earth. All this depends on me selling a couple of
paintings. Raising the funds to fly you out here and BLOW
FRANCIS COPPOLA'S MIND. I never liked him and he
never liked me. That is beside the point. I want you to have
a small cameo role in "ON THE ROAD." They all think I am
crazy and wild. His world is not my world. The intelligent
thing is to avoid people you do not like. What, am I going
crazy? Why should we enrich that stupid Guinea's life. Why
does he or his stupid friends deserve to see your magnifi-
cent gifts (body, mind & soul) They live such protected lives.
They are not even in the same room with you. We will use
the opposite tact and cunning. We will charm them to death
(the pants off their ass) We will dress immaculately and at
the proper moment spring the trap and blow their minds off
the PLANET EARTH
　　　We will do the great dance
　　　The great song
　　　The POEM
　　　We will be the essence of what creation is
　　　The main thing is the Act of CREATION
　　　The doing and the deed is the Revolution
YOU KNOW SWEETHEART
　　　I am poor and crazy
　　　I am a madman or woman
　　　I am the fly in your ointment
　　　A monkey on a stick
　　　A pumping cock pointed at the stars
　　　Ready to spurt firecracker to all the constellations!

We will emasculate their minds. Why does the establishment deceive you Amelia? Tell me ten reasons. Give me ten. These people are tatooed forever! We need to do it to those safe, monied, boring bastards. We need to pull them off their safe foundations. Why should you shine your gifts on them. He never commissioned me to write a movie. He's never accepted the rare gift of a great poet. He's a fucking American in his own home town. He's a epitomy of a still photo. The ghost of Lawrence Ferlinghetti. They both are senile in a pickled wino bottle. These people never grow, never, forever never grow!

Fuck them Amelia! Fuck them all Amelia! SHOULD WE SPRING A TRAP ON THEM? SHOULD WE BLOW THEIR MINDS. They are ghosts of time. Dead Images! Old Newspapers. Still Photos.

I am in a dilemma. I don't know what to do. I'd rather slip my tongue on your slippie-zippee. Fuck fame sweetheart. It is so fleeting. This stupid thing called fame. (power, money) There is no one here to play with my cock or balls. There is no one to hold hands with me. I have never been to the opera. I live in a small furnished room in a hotel. I am not part of the establishment. I never will be. It is all screwy and crazy world. It is such a stupid and crazy world. Why am I writing these stupid words on paper at 4:55 am 2 January 1995? Because I don't know a fucking thing about this world. Because I am an innocent babe. Because I am a child with a wild ego. A spoiled child on a wild ride. We are mischievous children. We are the world. That is why I drink scotch and ginger ale. A sweet and sour drink mixed. The heads and tail of a penny equals the 69 position in the sky. I must be a brilliant genius and I am already mad. Maybe I am both. Yes indeed!

Enclosed is my New Song; PISSER FOR TRUTH. A copy of my cat book. Please do a four or six line for each cat. Story-description-poetic imagination. Amelia, do your thing. We will do our own thing, Sweetheart. All I ask is your friendship. I cannot lead you to the Promised Land. I cannot open the gate for you. I cannot even open the gate for myself. All I can offer you is my friendship, my eyes, and tortured brain. I am fading in the twilight of my life and years. I want to blow their fucking minds so bad I can taste it. Should we go for all the marbles of time? Or just take a walk and laugh at the moon? The choice is ours! Those bastards of The Establishment give you nothing! They have nothing to give us. They have already sold out! Let's continue to be. To accept the world and be true to ourselves and work in small ways. Like true teachers and servants of a higher spirit. I've made my decision. This world needs a BIG ENEMA! If they do not know who they are let them pay for their indiscretions. Let them pay heavy for their unkindness. For their fucking greed. We don't need them. They need us so bad. They don't even know it.

Fuck them all
The long
And the short
And the tall
Fuck all the bastards
And their bastard Sons
Fuck them All
The Long
         and the short
              and the tall.
I am happy
I am crazy
I am wild
I am delirious
I am your friend
It is a great honor to be your friend Amelia
To be or not to be?
Give me your mind
Give me your love
Give me your advice
And your tongue
Give it all to me
Lay that sonnet on my heart
Lay it on totally all the way
And above all your eyes
Laughing at the moon
Sing me a song Sweetheart
Lay it on Babe and I'll love you forever
Beautiful animal

Beautiful wild thing
I love you forever my sweet
I need your pumping heart
I need your love
Whoppee Zippee

January 2, 1995-1900

ONE OF A KIND WAS PRINTED & BOUND IN AN EDITION OF ONE THOUSAND FIVE
HUNDRED COPIES BY MCNAUGHTON & GUNN OF SALINE, MICHIGAN.

THE FIRST FIVE HUNDRED COPIES CONTAIN A POSTER REPRODUCTION OF JACK
MICHELINE'S DIPOLE SERIES, COMMISIONED BY CHARLES WEHRENBERG.

THE COVERS WERE DESIGNED BY WILL YACKULIC WITH DIGITAL LAYOUT BY
JEREMY MICKEL & PRINTED AT POLYPRINT & DESIGN IN MANHATTAN.

BACK COVER PHOTOGRAPH BY MICHELLE MARIA BOLEYN,
SAN FRANCISCO, NINETEEN EIGHTY-FIVE.

THE TEXT IS SET IN CENTURY EXPANDED LT STANDARD AND THE TITLES ARE IN
CENTURY OLD STYLE STANDARD. DESIGN BY SOA WITH VISIONARY ASSISTANCE
FROM JP.

ONE OF A KIND IS NUMBER SIX IN UGLY DUCKLING PRESSE'S LOST LITERATURE
SERIES. THE LOST LITERATURE SERIES IS DEDICATED TO PUBLISHING NEGLECTED
WORKS OF 20TH CENTURY POETRY AND PROSE, AND IMPORTANT & RESONANT
WORKS THAT FALL OUTSIDE THOSE CONFINES.

THIS VOLUME WAS COMPILED & EDITED BY JULIEN POIRIER.
THE SERIES EDITOR IS RYAN HALEY.

OTHER TITLES IN THE SERIES INCLUDE:

SAINT GHETTO OF THE LOANS BY GABRIEL POMERAND (TRANS., M. KASPER)

ZERO TO NINE: THE COMPLETE MAGAZINE (EDS., V. ACCONCI & B. MAYER)

COMPLETE MINIMAL POEMS BY ARAM SAROYAN (ED., J. HOFF)

THE DEVELOPMENT OF AERIAL MILITARISM AND THE DEMOBILIZATION OF
EUROPEAN GROUND FORCES, FORTRESSES, AND NAVAL FLEETS
BY PAUL SCHEERBART (TRANS., M. KASPER)

EAST SLOPE BY SU SHI (TRANS., J. YANG)